Out of the
DARKNESS...
"Freedom Within"

Out of the
DARKNESS...
"Freedom Within"

Behind Prison Walls Within and Without

Joyce A. Leonard

Out of the Darkness... "Freedom Within"

Copyright © 2023 by Joyce A. Leonard. All rights reserved.

No part of this publication may be reproduced, stored in a retrieval system or transmitted in any way by any means, electronic, mechanical, photocopy, recording or otherwise without the prior permission of the author except as provided by USA copyright law.

The opinions expressed by the author are not necessarily those of URLink Print and Media.

1603 Capitol Ave., Suite 310 Cheyenne, Wyoming USA 82001
1-888-980-6523 | admin@urlinkpublishing.com

URLink Print and Media is committed to excellence in the publishing industry.

Book design copyright © 2023 by URLink Print and Media. All rights reserved.

Published in the United States of America
Library of Congress Control Number: 2023919892
ISBN 978-1-68486-624-3 (Paperback)
ISBN 978-1-68486-642-7 (Digital)

05.09.23

Acknowledgements

I am so grateful to Pauline Nota for her dedication in support of the Prison Ministry and calling me to share in the experience with her of serving those behind bars living within the confines of cement walls. Some of whom had lost family and friends due to their crimes but more than that they lost hope. It was the privilege of sharing in the ministry of "Freedom Within" to bring the hope of salvation to these men and women. Jesus gave His life for the worst of the worst and if there is breath there is hope for eternal life. We just wanted to give the opportunity and the recognition that all they had to do is receive the gift from God. It is free. This was a mission God placed on Pauline's heart and it was stirred in mine to join the divine calling and do the work that so many fail to recognize. "For God so loved the world that He gave His only begotten Son that whosoever should believe in Him, should not perish but have eternal life." (John 3:16)

My son, David Leonard Jr endured much throughout his life. He always had a willing heart to help others and give when he had nothing himself. Despite the circumstances of how he ended in prison, he never said a word against anyone else who had a hand in placing him there. He was thoughtful about the other person and their life. This was not always the case, but he met Jesus, and his heart was changed. He has always been my hero as I testified in a courtroom for him at his sentencing. He will tell you that his experience in prison prepared him to be the man that God wanted him to be. I am thankful for my son and the man he is.

To those who are named within the pages of this book, some still living and others that have died, I am indebted to have known them and their story. An accurate account is written in the books of heaven and God Who judges righteously, who created each of us in His image has an definite interest in each life for He shed His blood for them and He claims them as His children if they accept Him as Lord and Savior. To God be the glory now and forever. Amen.

Table of Contents

Introduction   Pages xv-xvii
Scripture Used: Isaiah 58:10-11
     Hebrews 13:3
     John 8:36

Chapter One   Origin of "Freedom Within"
     Pages 1-2
Scripture used: Matthew 5:6

Chapter Two   Pauline's Notes n' Quotes"
     Pages 3-19
     John 3:16
Sub – title: "Friendships"
     Mark 11:25
Sub-title: "Once a Marine Always a Marine"
     John 14:2-3 (NIV)
Sub-title   "Hard Rock Café vs Rock of Ages"
Sub-title: "Am I French or What?"
     John 15:2, Acts 10:3,
     Galatians 3:28; & 5:14-15
Sub-title: "False Witness"
     Exodus 20:16 (NKJV),
     Deuteronomy 19:15-2,
     Proverbs 6:16-19; 19:9; 20:28
     Isaiah 21:19 (NEB)
     Mathew 21:19; 28:60 (NEB)
     Exodus 23:1 (NIV)
     II Thessalonians 2:11 (NKJV)
     Proverbs 14:25 (NIV)
Sub-title: "Suffering and Pain"
     II Peter 2:9, Romans 8:8 (NKJV)

	James 1:2-3; 5:10-11 (NIV)
	I Peter 1:6-7 (NIV),
	Daniel 3:19-25, Acts 3:19
	I Peter 5:10-11 (NKJV)
Sub-title:	"Stop, Look and See"
	I John 1:9, Genesis 1:26
	I Corinthians 13:12 (NKJV)
Sub-title:	"Singing Drives Back the Power of Satan"
	Psalms 28:7, Exodus 32;18,
	Isaiah 66:23 (NLV)
	Zephaniah 3:17
Sub-title:	"Freedom Within and Without"
	Psalms 34:18 (NIV)
	Jeremiah 31:34, Micah 7:19,
	I John 1:9, Romans 8:2,
	John 8:32
Sub-title:	"One Lord, One Faith, One Baptism"
	Acts 3:38, I Corinthians 5:17
	Philippians 1:6, Mark16:16,
	Matthew 28:29
Sub-title:	"Wake-up Call'
	Isaiah 13:11, Genesis 6:5-7
	Genesis 18-19 (referenced)
	Matthew 24 (referenced)
	Joshua 1:9
Chapter Three	"Behind These Walls"
	Pages 20-45
Poem:	"Reflections in the Mirror"
Sub-title:	"Master Craftsman"
Sub-title:	"Types of Prisons"
	Hebrews 13:3,
	Jeremiah 33:3 (referenced)
	Isaiah 40:3
Sub-title:	"Brotherly or Sisterly Love"
	I John 2:3-5, 6-7, 3:15-18 (KJV)

Out of the Darkness... "Freedom Within"

	I John 4:4
Sub-title:	"Media Declaration vs. Defended"
Sub-title:	"Which Direction Reflects Jesus"
Sub-title:	"A Karios Experience"
Sub-title:	"Too Long Separated from Him"
	James 5:6
Sub-title:	"New Beginnings"
	Romans 12:1-2 (KJV).
	Romans 1:8,12, 1:15, ch. 9-11 (referenced)
	II Corinthians 1:3, Philippians 2:1
	Colossians 3:12, Hebrews 10:28
	Matthew 9:16, Romans 1:25
	I Peter 1:4, Hebrews 1:2,
	Matthew 17:2, Mark 9:22,
	Romans 12:2, II Corinthians 4:16
	Colossians 3:10, Hebrews 6:6.
	Ephesians 4:23
Sub-title:	"Fellowship"
Sub-title:	"Christ at the Helm"
Sub-title:	"The Perfect Friend"
	Romans Chap. 7 referenced.
Sub-title:	"Revival"
Sub-title:	"Prison Life"
Sub-title:	"Human Instincts"
Sub-title:	"A Dream or Reality"
Chapter Four	"Prisoners of Hope"
	Pages 47- 76
Poem:	"Thoughts in the Night" by Kevin Tardiff
Sub- title"	"Testimony of Tony Abreau"
	Hebrews 13:20-21
Sub-title:	"Testimony of Jimmy Wood"
	Romans 10:9-10, 13, I John 1:9
	Mark 9:23, Philippians 4:13
	Romans 12:1-2, II Peter 2:9
	II Peter 3:9

Poem: "Hello God" by Jerry Larrivee
Drawings by Dennis Lennon pgs. 54
Photo and drawings by Dennis Lennon pg 54
Poem by Stephen Mickey pg. 55
"Confession by James Brown Lewis"
Letter from Zambia, So. Africa pgs. 56-57
                  Romans 8:28, Romans 8:1
Sub-title: "The Master Craftsman" by Pryor Hall pgs. 58-60
                  James 1:22-23, Isaiah 55:8-11
                  Acts 17:23, Matthew 5:3-4
                  Romans 1:21, Revelation 3:1-3
                  Genesis 8:1, Jeremiah 18:1-11
                  I Corinthians 13:13, I John 4:8
                  Micah 7:7-8, John 3:16
Poem: "Prisoner's are Forgotten" by Joseph French
Sub-title: "Thoughts from David Jack" pg. 61
Drawing (Anonymous) "Prisoner of Hope"
                  Psalms 107:10-16
Poem: "Keep Your Faith" by Timothy Sanders
Testimony by Frank C. pgs. 63-64
                  John 3;3, John 3:16
Sub-title: "Coerced Confession" by Bobby Moore Jr.
Sub-title: "The Magician" by Jeffrey Brent Hannah pg. 66
Sub-title: "Holiday Spirit" by Jerry Larrivee
Sharing "My Lessons Learned" by Jeff Hannah
"Alethea's Hope and Prayer" pg. 69
Quotes from Inmates"
Poem: "Keep Your Head Up" by Wilfred Clark
Sub-title: "Only he Strong Survive" by Eric Calvin
Drawing by Eric Calvin – pg. 72
Sub-title   "A Second Chance"
Sub-title: "Testimony of Robert Clark"
                  Revelation 12:11

Sub-title: "Choose How to Start Your Day Tomorrow"
Matthew 6:34
Drawing by Michael Clark
Quote – pg. 76

Chapter Five: "RAGE" Pages 77-83
Matthew 22:37; 19:19; 19:26
Philippians 4:13

Chapter Six   "From the Halls of Death Row"
Pages 84-101

Sub-title: "Cruelty Within the Walls of Death Row"
Sub-title: "If You Support Capital Punishment"
Sub-title: "The American Holocaust"
Sub-titles: "Executions" pg. 92-94
Luke 1:78-79 (NRSV)
Sub-title: "Methods of Execution"
Drawing by Unknown Death-Row Inmate
"Obituary of Bobby Ray Hopkins"
Sub-title: "Mumia Abu Jamal"
Poem "Hell on Earth" by Kevin Tardiff
Drawing "Death Awaits" by Stanley Wetmore

Chapter Seven   "Attention Public Hearing" Pages 102-104

Chapter Eight   "Inside and Out" Pages 105-111
Sub-title: "Police Procedures"
Sub-title: "Life in Maximum Security – Super Max"
Sub-title: "Incarceration Rates"
Poem: "The Love of God" by Frederick M. Lehman 1917

Chapter Nine   "Memorials" Pages 112-118

Chapter Ten   "Penned from Joyce in 'Freedom Within' Newsletters" Pages 119
Isaiah 61:1, Luke 19:1-19
Sub-titles: "Friendship Debt"

Joyce A. Leonard

                John 15:13, II Corinthians 9:7
                Ecclesiastes 9:10 (NIV)
Poem: "Flowering… Fading… Friendships"
Sub-title: "You are Invited."
                Luke 14:15-24, Christ's Object Lessons by
                EG White pg. 123
Sub-title: "To Vow or Not to Vow."
                Joshua 24:14-15, Numbers 30:2-3
                Psalms 96:11, Ecclesiastes 5:4-5
                John 14:1-3, I John 1:9, Isaiah 42:59
                Matthew 25:21
Poem "The Beauty" pg. 126
Sub-title: "The Christian of Love or
                The Tare of Hypocrisy"
                Jeremiah 17:9, Matthew 19:24-31; 13:36-43
                Hebrews 10:24-25
Sub-title: "Hoodwinked Again."
                Matthew 5:46, 6:14-15; Romans 13:14-20
                II Thessalonians 1:6, Hebrews 11:25-26
                Ecclesiastes 2:11, Luke 23:34, John 3:16
Sub-title: "As Time Goes On."
                Philippians 4:11, Matthew 6:19-21
Sub-title: "The Effects of Pain"
                Psalms 139:14, I Samuel 18:31
                Psalms 56:8 (KJV), Luke 8:16-39
                Hebrews 8:1, I Peter 4:12-13
                II Thessalonians 1:6, Hebrews 10:30,
                John 3:15-17, I John 5:14-16,
Galatians 5:22-23
Poem: "I Love You So '
                Matthew 27:51a- 52b
                Matthew 5:45
Sub-title: "Penned from Joyce."
Sub-title: "Forever Too Late"
                James 3:8, Proverbs 15:1,
                Ecclesiastes 5:2, Proverbs 29:20

Sub-title:	II Chronicles 20:8, Isaiah 65:2, Ephesians 6:20; 4:26-20 "Have You Grown Weary With Your Praying?" Luke 22:31; 22:40, Hebrews 3:7; 7:25 James 1:16, Isaiah 59:1; 55:8-9 Job 12:2-4,; 13:5
Sub-title:	"Thy Will Be Done, Lord" Jeremiah 33:3, Psalms 17:8, Philippians 2:13, III John 2 John 3:18, Numbers 23:19
Chapter Eleven	"Let's Get it Right." Pages 141-144
Chapter Twelve	"A Place of refuge" Pages 148-154 Psalms 31:2, Numbers 19; 35:12-15 Leviticus 11:44, I Peter 1:16, John 6:37, I Peter 5:8, I John 3:16-18
Chapter Thirteen: Sub-title:	"Freedom Promised" Pages 155-161 "Risky Business" I John 2:25, John 3:16
Sub-Title: Sub-title:	"Straight Talk" by Michael Braiser "Behind These Bars" by Robert Salo
Chapter Fourteen:	"Freedom Promised" – Part II Pages 162-167
Sub-Title	"The Price of Mischief" Proverbs 6:18; 10:23
Sub-title:	"Behind These Bars" by Robert Salo II Corinthians 6:14-16
Chapter Fifteen	"The Power of a Badge" Pages 168-172 Psalms 97:10, Psalms 11:7

Chapter Sixteen: "Hope During a Time of Hopelessness"
Pages 173-177
Jeremiah 29:11, Matthew 25:23

Chapter Seventeen: "Justice vs Injustice"
Pages 178-182
Ecclesiastes 3:14-15

Chapter Eighteen: "There is a Target on Your Back"
Pages 183-191
II Peter 2:9, Luke 18:7-8
Isaiah 58:7-8

***Note:** Bible versions used
KJV = King James Version
NKJV= New King James Version
NIV = New International Version
NLT=New Living Translation
NRS= New Revised Standard

Introduction

"If you pour out that which you sustain your own life for the hungry and satisfy the need of the afflicted, then shall your light rise in the darkness, and your obscurity and gloom become like the noonday. And the Lord shall guide you continually and satisfy you in drought in and in dry places and make strong your bones. And you shall be like a watered garden and like a spring of water whose waters fail not."
(Isaiah 58:10-11)

Darkness manifests itself in many forms. It presents itself to the lonely, the discouraged, those who have been rejected and have no where to go. Darkness is a tool of the enemy, and it brings out the worst in those who find themselves in that pit of despair to do the unthinkable things toward others and to themselves. It usually derives from somewhere along the lines of rejection from a parent, a spouse, or children. It grows into a wall of hatred and bitterness that eats at your soul and turns it into a turmoil of frenzy. Even if you were brought up a Christian and had wonderful caring parents, the prince of darkness, Satan, himself has devised a plan to destroy even those who think they may be free of such heinous acts of crime or despicable things that they find themselves involved in and then things like addiction follow the broken ones that want relief in any form available.

Then the flip side of the coin shows that pride, envy, and deceitfulness filtered with endless lies bring another type of darkness at your doorstep. Money and wealth are especially a snare for the greedy in heart and looking for their own benefit. All these things will come forward in the pages ahead. Some never made it to a judge and jury so you are now the jury for those incidents. When the verdict is in where do you stand for or against? There is a judgment seat right now waiting for each of us and there is an accurate account being kept by holy angels. Which side are you on, and which way will you walk?

"Freedom Within" was a newsletter sent out to prisons throughout the United States, Canada, Mexico, and Africa. It grew for five years until financial needs of a copy machine and a divorce for Joyce and her health issues came into play. The logo is captured on the front page of this book. The verse we sent to bring hope was "If the Son sets you free, you shall be free indeed." (John 8:36) We are all in need of such freedom and we long for it. *"Remember the prisoners as if chained with them – those who are mistreated - since you yourselves are in the body also." (Hebrews 13:3)*

"Freedom Within" was born with 185 copies first issued to the Maine State Prison through the acceptance and dispensing of Matt Kantrowitz, the prison chaplain. It soon became popular, not just within the prison population but outside the prison walls, others began to ask for it to be sent to them. The total excelled to 250 and being dispersed among several states.

When the outreach began the little table model copy machine could handle 150 copies of 4 pages on both sides but advancing to 250 copies and five pages both sides made the newsletter a 10-page letter. The school department that Joyce worked for granted her to use their copy machine one time for $15. Joyce kept asking the secretary at the Administration office one more time and each time she reluctantly allowed the copying to continue but with a definite disgruntled look on her face. A prayer was breathed for the machine to be able to continue, and God provided for that to continue until it reached 500 copies and soon the demand became greater and now it was up to 900. Pauline took it to the church Conference office, and they allowed a onetime printing free of charge, it was a struggle to find a copy machine to keep up with the demand. But God was good! Each time something came through and the copies grew to 1500. Soon we acquired a copy machine that was donated to us and kept within Joyce's home. That kept going serving many prisons throughout various places in the US and other countries previously mentioned. Now it was up to 2500 copies. This continued for 5 years until our coping machine broke down and there were not enough financial means to keep it going along with home & health that plummeted Joyce into major back surgery. The pages ahead are an experience I am glad that I was able to be a part of and now to tell our story and the story of those that have come out of the darkness to "Freedom Within."

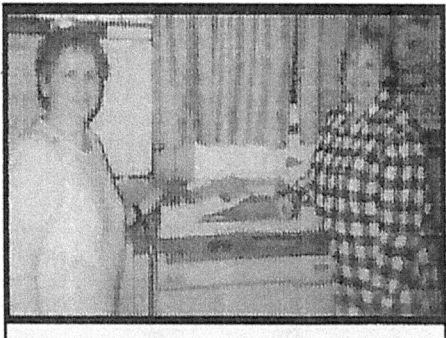

Joyce Leonard & Pauline Nota
in front of Lanier 6745 Copier

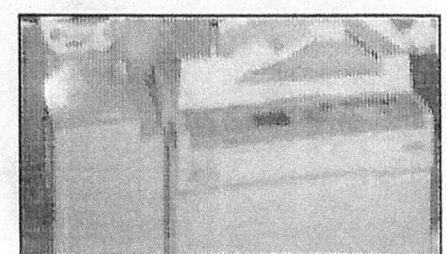

Lanier 6745 Copier

Origin of Freedom Within

*"Blessed are they which do hunger
and thirst after righteousness for they shall be filled"
(Matthew 5:6 NKJV).*

CHAPTER ONE

February 18, 1997, Pauline Nota was sitting in the pastor's office at the Seventh-day Adventist Church on 316 Minot Ave. in Auburn, ME when Pastor Ken Baumgarten passed her a letter. It was from the Maine State Prison. He didn't just pass it to Pauline because she was there. "No." Pauline had a passion to reach souls closed in behind bars, to let them know there was hope…there is "freedom within" prisons. Freedom within the mind and peace can be obtained. The pastor knew this.

Pauline had been searching out ideas and avenues to enter into a ministry within prisons. It seemed to be difficult to make an entrance when there is clergy already available to inmates. Pauline didn't want to provide clergy that was already provided but to encourage and enhance a desire to be reborn. Those who are already reborn she wanted to provide a little TLC for those hungering in their search. She wanted to work with the clergy already available to be supportive in a team ministry.

The letter she opened and read was a steppingstone toward the newsletter "Freedom Within" as well as it advanced to this book which continues the ministry after all these years and has developed into another phase of the outreach.

It was a letter from an inmate at the Maine State Prison, a soul searching for acceptance within a Christian community. Pauline responded with eagerness to Roland Dube's need for food and clothing through the Community Service Center of our church.

This became an ongoing correspondence that developed into a real friendship between Pauline and Roland, and they became brother and sister of faith linked by Jesus Christ and His love abounding in both of their lives.

Each week Pauline brought the request to her church family to pray for Roland and his needs. Bits and pieces unfolded and a few fervent prayer warriors including the pastor became more and more familiar with Roland. She began to send the church newsletter called the Auburn Accolade to Roland. I added my photo being the editor of the church newsletter. My picture awakened Roland's memory when he had known a young woman briefly 25 years ago at that time and it was me!

Roland related his story to Pauline, who in turn had inquired of me if it were true. I was in awe. Yes – it was true. It was then Roland and I reunited through correspondence. A friendship that hallows the ground of friendship had been rekindled. That brief friendship marked a significant difference in my life and also left a lasting impression on Roland. One that had stayed embedded in his memory for 25 years.

When I learned of Roland's circumstances, I felt he had suffered from unjust, unfair events, yet he was now a Christian transformed by the Holy Spirit, and became a brother in Christ. I realized this unfairness was allowed to bring hope to others who are sincere in their search of peace, truth and truly desiring "freedom within."

The prison ministry began but the newsletter had not taken place yet. Pauline was in her kitchen praying about the inmates she had met at Maine State Prison asking God to speak to her concerning a newsletter. Clearly and audibly, she heard the voice say, "Freedom Within." She knew immediately that was to be the name of the newsletter and it was ordained by God. She asked me to be part of this ministry since I had already begun praying for inmates as well as I was the editor of the church newsletter. There was a mishap within the church concerning the church newsletter and I retired from that job allowing God to plunge me into the prison ministry newsletter.

Pauline's Notes and Quotes

*"For God so loved the world that He
gave His only begotten Son that
whosoever believes in Him should not
perish but have everlasting life."
(John 3:16 NKJV)*

CHAPTER TWO

"Has your friend hurt you or betrayed you? Has your friend falsely accused you? Has your friend taken your friendship lightly or even for granted? Has your friend been manipulative or possessive? Is your friend really not your friend but merely an acquaintance?

Friendship is something we all crave and without it we feel isolated. It was quoted that "No man is an island.' (Poem written by John Donne 1582-1631 London England) and "the world is a stage, and the people are all actors" (first written by Shakespeare). As time progresses in my life, I believe these statements are very true. In a lifetime we may only claim a handful of really true friends.

True friends are gifts from God, and we should treasure them, "Treasure is not always a friend, but a friend is always a treasure." (*Chi trova un amico trova un tesoro* also known as *A Friend Is a Treasure*) If you don't feel you have one true friend, then ask yourself if you yourself are a true friend to someone else. To have a friend, you must be a friend. "There is no scale or chart on earth to measure what a true friend is worth."

I have experienced many disappointments with people I thought were friends. I have been hurt many times and it is not always easy to forgive, but my Bible tells me that if I don't forgive, I won't be forgiven by God. (See Mark 11:25) These are very strong words, and it could cost a person their salvation, but God makes it possible to forgive so that we so have hope. There is one friend that I have that has never disappointed me, in fact, He actually died for me. His name is Jesus, and I want to share Him with each of you. He will never use you or take you for granted. He loves you unconditionally, just the way you are. All you have to do is believe in Him and accept Him into your heart and He will be your friend."

(Taken from Vol. Issue 2 of "Freedom Within" 1998)

"One a Marine always a Marine"

"Are there any marines out there? This middle-aged lady was a Marine. The Marine Corps is an elite branch of the service and being part of it makes you feel like you are part of a huge military family. I had come from a wonderful and close-knit family and the Marine Corps just added another form off family to my life. It was quite an adventure and an experience I will never forget. After my boot training at Paris Island, SC, I was stationed at Camp Lejeune, NC. My next duty station was at Camp Smith in Hawaii, where I met my husband, whom I outranked at the time. We married and started our own family. Now I was part of my family, his family, the Marine Corps family & our family. Our son-in law was an officer in the Marine Corps, and we are definitely a patriotic family.

From the end of May to the 4th of July we celebrate Memorial Day, Flag Day and Independence Day and we should be proud to be Americans. I still get a thrill when I see "Old Glory" go by in the parade. I also put flags on graves, and it doesn't matter if they were veterans or not, but what matters is that they were Americans. In spite of the corrupt politicians, this country is still the freest country in the world. No matter if you are incarcerated you still are an American and you can also appreciate the freedom of religion and speech among other benefits not realized by other inmates in other countries.'

"I think of all the blood that was shed to keep our land free and the American Flag born June 14, 1777, is a symbol of that freedom. The cross is another symbol of shed blood to make us all free. When Jesus shed His precious blood on that cross, He gave us the opportunity of becoming a member of the family of God. This is the best family of all and no matter what your family life has been like you can belong to this family now and forever. God loves us unconditionally and He wants everyone of us to belong to His family.

All we have to do is accept Jesus into our hearts and believe that He died for us and that He was resurrected. When He comes back for us, He will bring us to His home where we can spend eternity as members of God's family. Jesus said, "In My Father's house are many rooms, and if it were not so I would have told you. And if I go and prepare a place for you, I will come back and take you to be with Me that you may also be where I am." (John 14:2-3 NIV) Will you enjoy the mansion that Jesus has prepared for you or will someone else?"

(Taken from Volume 1, Issue 3 of "Freedom Within" 1998)

Note: We recognize the service of other branches of the service and their dedication in serving our country to keep it a place of freedom. We are blessed by all services of the military to protect our country."

Pauline describes her adventures from her trip to North Carolina.

"I just returned to Maine from North Carolina after spending three months in North Carolina making wonderful memories with my daughter while her husband, who is an officer in the Marine Corps, had been deployed to Turkey. Although I am happy to be back, I did not miss the Maine winters. On my extended vacation, I was able to further "Freedom Within" Prison outreach to Florida, No. Carolina, and So. Carolina. I was able to visit an inmate in each of these states. Through a speaking engagement and other contacts, I was able to add many names to our pen-friend program, which means many more inmates will be receiving mail. The 'Freedom Within' newsletter is now being distributed to 923 people and our goal is to reach every prison in the United States. We are also in one prison in Africa.

Myrtle Beach, NC was one of my favorite places to visit and although the places and entertainment we experienced was wonderful, I thought I would share with you my first experience at the 'Hard Rock Café.' The structure of the main building was such a magnificent structure. In the world-wide family of Hard Rock Cafes this one is the only one that is shaped like a pyramid shape because they claim, like the ancient pyramids, rock music is timeless and has the power to transcend time, cultures, and borders.

The exterior of the pyramid features a realistic ancient Egyptian motif with 1800-pound sphinxlike statues made of fiberglass, waterfalls, palm trees, and stone columns with hieroglyphics. The point at the top of the pyramid is eleven feet, 8" tall, weighs 2500 lbs. and is made of glass. The floor is 12'10" under the ground. The raised dining area measures approximately 2000 sq. ft. A unique time capsule, which preserves relics from some great names in a roll that is displayed within the pyramid. The Egyptian sarcophagus was sealed and dedicated at the site in May 1995 and will be opened 100 years after in the year 2095. Included is memorabilia from South Carolina's Hootie and the Blowfish, a brick from the original Cavern Club in Liverpool where the Beatles started their career, etc.

As I looked around the dining room, I noticed a waiter wearing sunglasses with bleach blonde hair tied up in a ponytail on top of his head wearing a nose ring! The music was very loud so while waiting for my food I decided to walk around the second level. There were all sorts of memorabilia from rock stars such as their pictures, clothes, and instruments. I saw guitars that belonged to Bob Dylan, Jerry Garcia, Jimmy Hendrix, and Carlos Santana. There were a set of drums from Guns n' Roses, a piano from Brian Wilson of the Beach Boys and Joan Jet's tennis shoes. There were numerous gold, silver, and platinum records hanging all over the walls. One very interesting item was a gold frame and where the pictures would have been where the words 'The Pope Smokes Dope.'

You are probably thinking you would like to see this place, but first let me tell you about the 'Rock of Ages Café,' that I created in my mind and see which one you would choose if Jesus were going with you.

In place of the Egyptian pharaoh facing, you as you walk in on a huge stained-glass window, I would have the depiction of Jesus with thousands of angels in the clouds as He will appear when He returns, as described in the Bible. In place of drums, I would recreate the 'Last Supper' scene. The loud rock music would be replaced with beautiful gospel music. I would replace that gold frame including the slogan about the Pope, with a replica of the 'Ten Commandments.' The waiters and waitresses would be dressed as Bible characters. In place of the sarcophagus, I would put a replica of the tomb of Christ to show the world that it is empty, and He lives. In place of the records, I would put copies of the Dead Sea Scrolls, which prove the authenticity of the Bible. On every table would be a Bible and Bible trivia questions and while waiting for their food, people could read and answer the questions.

The menu would be full of healthy delicious entrees and a salad bar would have lots of fresh vegetables and fruits. Fresh grape juice and bread would be served as a reminder of the 'Last Supper.' The piano would be replaced with one huge cross as a reminder of the price Jesus paid for us. In place of the worldly entertainment, there would be an angelic choir each evening.

It would be a beautiful, peaceful place where all would be welcome whether they could pay or not. I think you get the picture. Why do we insist on idolizing these rock stars who were mere human beings? Why must we make heroes of them with their immoral behavior? Because they are Satan's most powerful tools to influence the younger generation. Think why you were incarcerated today and the influence these rock stars had on you. They sing about drugs and alcohol, suicide and murder, sexual perversion which is the way they live and die. The only hero is Jesus, and His example speaks for itself. He gave His life for each one of us unconditionally. The rock stars live luxurious lives in the fast lane, but how many of them are happy? They and you can only find true happiness in Jesus Christ, the Rock of Ages. Yes, only Jesus is timeless with the power to transcend time, not rock music. Now which do you chose?"

(Taken from Volume 2, Issue 2 of "Freedom Within" 1999)

Joyce A. Leonard

"Am I French or What?"

"Yes, I am certainly French, and I am very proud of my heritage. My dad's family was from France and my mom's family from Canada, and I couldn't ask for a more enriched way of life than the culture I was raised in. I particularly enjoyed the wonderful French cooking and all the traditions I grew up with and I am passing on to my family. Being bilingual has also been a plus for me and I've used my French in Rome and Israel.

Many people have not been as fortunate as I was and had to deal with much prejudice. I don't appreciate the French jokes and even though some of us have French accents, it doesn't make us any less intelligent than anyone else. I could never understand why some French people actually changed their names so that others wouldn't know they were French. Today in the Lewiston/Auburn area of Maine, where I live, the French have finally claimed back their French heritage and the pride is back and we can now speak our language proudly even in public. In the past when visiting an elderly aunt in a boarding home, I was asked not to speak French with her.

We were in our own space and not being rude by speaking French in front of non-French speaking people. This was very offensive to me as I thought we lived in a free country!

What about you? Have you experienced prejudice in your various cultures, races, or ethnic backgrounds? I believe that everyone should be proud of their heritage no matter if they are yellow, white, black, or brown. God is a God of color and He made us all in His image. As I look at the awesome rainbows and the flowers that He created I can't help but appreciate that if everyone or everything was one color, it would be a very boring world.

I enjoy all my brothers and sisters of different races and beliefs and I really enjoy learning and sharing with them. We are all God's children, and we must learn to love one another as He loved us. (See John 15:12) Jewish people have always been a particular target for discrimination and how ironic that God chose this particular race for His Son to be born into. What race would you have chosen for Him? Most people would probably have preferred Him to have chosen their own race, thence derives the reason for so much disharmony and discord in this very prejudice world.

'Even His own people turned against Him and yet in Acts 10:3, Peter said, 'In truth I perceive that God shows no partiality.'

The problem is that most people feel that if other people were different than they are, that they are not as good as them. People who feel this way are insecure and ignorant. Many people discriminate against people who have different sexual preferences, different religions, different nationalities and even against people who are handicapped! What I can't understand is if people want others to be like them, why do men want to be women and women want to be men? Why do black people want to be white, and whites want to be black? Why are they so prejudiced against each other while imitating their style of dressing? Why are the darker blacks prejudiced against the lighter black people and vice versa?

To God it really doesn't matter why the world is so prejudiced against each other for we are all His sons and daughters. In Galatians 3:28, Paul said, 'There is neither Jew nor Greek, there is neither slave nor free, there is neither male nor female, for you are all one in Christ Jesus.' We will be judged by God as to how we treat our brothers and sisters. 'For all the law is filled with one word, even in this: you shall love your neighbor as yourself.' 'But if you bite and devour one another, beware lest you be consumed by one another!' (Galatians 5:14-15) Let's all make this world a better place to live in by loving and treating one another as we would want to be loved and treated."

(Taken from Volume 2 Issue 3 of "Freedom Within" 1999)

"The False Witness"

"Someone once said, 'When you hear more than one account of an accident, then you begin to worry about history,' A witness is someone who saw something and gave a firsthand account of it. Witnesses testify under oath in court. They will also be present at the signing of documents and attest to the event by attaching their signatures. Naturally, we want to know that witness is true and honest.

The problem of false witnesses, however, it seems to go back to the beginning of time. Otherwise, why would the ninth commandment read 'You shall not bear false witness against your neighbor.' (Exodus 20:16 NKJV) The Deuteronomic code had specific and severe instructions for dealing with perjury (See Deuteronomy 19:15-21), as most of us can testify, bearing false witness has been an ongoing problem with the human race.

The wise men of the Bible had to speak of perjury: 'The Lord hates…a false witness who pours out lies.' (Proverbs 6:16-19 NIV) 'A false witness will not go unpunished.' (Proverbs 19:9) A false witness will perish and whoever listens to him will be destroyed forever.' (Proverbs 21:28 NIV) And whoever 'by falsehood [denies] justices to the righteous…will be exterminated.' (Isaiah 29:21 NEB) These are strong words. In addition, we need to add all the false prophets and diviners who fabricated messages, visions, and dreams to delude believers.

Jesus listed perjury in horrific list of sins that proceeds from the heart…{and} defile a man." (Matthew 15:19 NEB) False witnesses participated in His trial (Matthew 28:60). The same people paid for and setup false witnesses against Stephen, the first Christian martyr (Acts 6:13 NKJV).

To become a malicious witness, an instrument of evildoers, is risky business (Exodus 23:1 NIV). Paul makes the chilling observation that deceivers will have a strong delusion, that they should believe a lie" (2 Thessalonians 2:11 NKJV). They will in fact, reach a point where they can't know whether they are telling the truth or not.

A wise man put it simply: "A truthful witness saves lives." (Proverbs 14:25 NIV) Christ Himself is supreme true witness."

Jesus in you I find the perfect faithful witness. Give me the patience to endure those times when others have spoken falsely against me. (Taken from Glimpses of God by Dorothy Minchin-Comm)

(Taken from Volume 2 Issue 4 of "Freedom Within 1999)

"Suffering and Pain"

No one is exempt from suffering and pain, and we all have our crosses to carry. How do we handle our suffering and pain? Some suffer in silence, and some complain while some through their faith in a loving God, and put it in God's hands. No matter how much we suffer, we could never suffer as much as Jesus did in his short life here on earth. He actually volunteered to be brutally murdered in a slow cruel extremely painful way. All this to save us and assure us a place where there will be no more suffering and pain.

In the book, "Desire of Ages" pg. 528, my favorite author, Ellen White, writes 'To all who are reaching out to feel the guiding hand of God, the moment of greatest discouragement is the time when divine help is nearest. They look back with thankfulness on the darkest part of their way. 'The Lord knows how to deliver the godly.' (2 Peter 2:9) From every trial He will bring them forth with firmer faith and richer experience. 'So, I tell you, through my own experiences with suffering and pain, that I can certainly accept it more readily, 'for I consider that the sufferings of this present time are not worthy to be compared with the glory that shall be revealed in us.' (Romans 8:18)

God will not allow us to suffer more than we are able to bear, but the next six scriptures will explain why we will continue to suffer while we are in this world. 'Consider it pure joy, my brothers, whenever you face trials of many kinds, because you know that the testing of your faith develops perseverance.' (James 1:2 & 3) 'Brothers as an example of patience in the face of suffering, take the prophets who spoke in the name of the Lord. As you know, we consider blessed those who have persevered. You have heard of Job's perseverance and seen what the Lord finally brought about. The Lord is full of compassion and mercy.' (James 5:10-11) 'In this you greatly rejoice, though now for a little while you may have had to suffer grief in all kinds of trials. These have come so your faith – may be proved genuine and may result in praise, glory, and honor when Jesus is revealed.' (I Peter 1:6,7)

The following are a few excellent quotes on suffering: 'God permits what He hates in order to achieve what He loves' (Quoted by Steve Estes in the book, 'When God Weeps'). 'Suffering is having what we don't want and wanting what we don't have' (quote by Elizabeth Elliot). 'Pray that you will never have to bear all that you are able to endure.' (Jewish Proverb)

Dorothy Minchin-Comm wrote the following in 'Glimpses of God,' and it sums up what I feel about the first question we ask is 'Why?' 'Why me?' 'I don't deserve it.' The more Christian inquiry is 'Why not me?' 'Is there any reason why I should be exempt from the human lot of suffering?' God however doesn't always take us out of the problems. Sometimes He enters in with us- as he joined the three exiles in Nebuchadnezzar's fiery furnace (See Daniel 3:19-25). Jesus is our model. His rejection, pain and suffering worsened, ending only at the cross. As Peter pointed out in his sermon at Solomon's portico, the full spectrum of suffering and misery was 'thus fulfilled.' (Acts 3:18)

She who was a widow knows how to comfort the girl whose bridegroom was killed by a drunken driver, a month after their wedding. He who has been unjustly imprisoned will know what another victim of corruption needs to hear. Parents who have lost a child will be the first to step forward when the child down the street is abducted. Can it be that suffering is part of our necessary education in our highly imperfect world? Is it the means that enables us to help another toward the kingdom?

I include her beautiful prayer, 'Help me, God, to remember that my suffering, whatever it may be, is only temporary. It may be a day, a week, a year. Or even to the day I die. But freedom and joy lie beyond.' My prayers are with you all and I leave you with I Peter 5:10 & 11, 'But may the God of all grace, who called us to His eternal glory by Christ Jesus, after you have suffered awhile, perfect, establish, strengthen, and settle you. To Him be the glory and the dominion forever and ever. Amen,'"

(Taken from Volume 3 Issue 1 "Freedom Within" 2000)

"Stop, Look and See!"

"What do you see when you look in the mirror? Do you see any changes in the face you have been looking at for years? Those approaching mid-life may see signs of aging but look beyond all that with your spiritual vision and now what do you see?

Stop, look, and see deep within yourself remembering that the Holy Spirit dwells within you. Do you see anger, hurt, frustration or pain? Maybe now you see joy, love, and peace. When a person accepts the Spirit of God in their hearts and surrenders totally to Him, the reflection in the mirror may very well be His reflection.

As Founder of the 'Freedom Within' Prison Outreach, God has put many inmates in my path through correspondence and visiting. I consider many of these inmates my friends, and I can see the face of Christ in many of them. Many are very strong in their faith and witnessing behind bars and I have been truly blessed by knowing them. Many are skeptical of inmates who profess to love the Lord and I do agree that there are many 'jailhouse' conversions, but I have personally witnessed some that are truly converted. We all fall from time to time, but if we do what it says in I John 1:9 we can go on as His faithful followers.

Stop, look, and see the Spirit of God in others an in ourselves, and see that we are fully made in His image (Genesis 1:26). 'For we now see in a mirror dimly, but then we will see face to face. Now I know in part then I will know fully, even as I have been fully known.' (I Corinthians 13:12) God bless you and may His Spirit dwell within you so you may experience 'Freedom Within.'"

(Taken from Volume 3 Issue 3 "Freedom Within" 2000)

Singing Drives Back the Power of Satan

"The Lord is my strength and my shield, my heart trusts in Him, and I am helped therefore my heart greatly rejoices, and with my song I will praise Him.'
(Psalms 28:7)

"I know many of you really enjoy singing and I pray that you will use your vocal gift that God has given you to sing praises to your beloved Savior. When ever I sing at a wedding, other functions or at the church, I always pick a hymn or spiritual song that touches my heart and then I ask the Lord to let it touch someone's heart. These hymns of praise are prayers that go to the throne of God and when I sing these songs from my heart, I feel so close to Him. The Bible says, 'It is not the voice of those who shout in victory, nor is it the voice of those who cry out in defeat, but the voice of those who sing that I hear.' (Exodus 32:18)

"The word sing is mentioned in the Bible about 116 times and that does not include the words, sang, singeth, singing and sung. Whenever something is mentioned numerous times in the Bible, it means it is very important. We do not have to have terrific voices to sing and praise the Lord. It is so easy to keep the beloved hymns we hear so often, in our hearts. We sing to ourselves or to others, and in almost any circumstances that we are in. I particularly like singing along with the cassette tapes when I am driving. When life gets the best of me, I put on my Gaither video tapes and I enjoy their beautiful gospel and Southern gospel songs. Their songs of praise uplift me, and life always seems so much brighter afterwards,"

"My favorite author Ellen G. White wrote, 'Christ took upon Him human nature, that He might be able to sympathize with all hearts… His Spirit was never full of worldly cares that He had no time for thought of the heavenly. He could give evidence of His cheerfulness by singing psalms and heavenly songs. The people of Nazareth often heard His voice raised in praise and thanksgiving to God. He often held communion with heaven in song, and all who were associated with Him, who often complained of their weariness of labor…were cheered by the melody that fell from His lips. His praises seemed to drive away the evil angels, and as incense, filled the room with sweet fragrance.'"

'This too had its lesson. It taught that people could commune with God in words of holy song. Christ carried the minds of his hearers away from their earthy exile to their future eternal home as songs of praise are sung, as fervent earnest prayers arise to heaven, as lessons are repeated of the wondrous works of God, as the heart's gratitude is expressed in prayer and song, angels from heaven take up the strain and unite in praise and thanksgiving to God.'

'These exercises drive back the power of Satan, they expel murmurings and complaints, and Satan loses ground. God teaches us that we should assemble in His house to cultivate the attributes of perfect love. This will fit the mansions of earth for the mansions Christ has gone to prepare for them that love Him. Then they will assemble in the sanctuary from Sabbath to Sabbath, from one New Moon to another, to unite in loftier strains of song, in thanksgiving, and praise to Him, Who sits on the throne, and to the Lamb forever and ever.' (Isaiah 66:23)

"I pray that we all will inhabit one of those beautiful mansions that Jesus has prepared for those who love Him, and that we can all join Him and His glorious choir of angels in songs of praise. But while we wait here on earth let us rejoice in lifting up our voices in songs of praise and worship till we meet with Him face to face where He will rejoice over you with singing,'" (See Zephaniah 3:17) {Taken from Volume 3 Issue 4 of "Freedom Within" 2000)

"Freedom Within and Without"

"Freedom is a basic human need…" Many of you are incarcerated and are no longer free to do as you please but remember that even people who are not locked up are in prison in one way or another are still imprisoned.

Some are unhappy in their marriages: some are imprisoned through illness whether mental or physical. Some are imprisoned through drug, alcohol, or sexual additions, and some are imprisoned through the guilt of past mistakes and sins. The good news is God can see us though all out enslavements. 'The Lord is close to the broken hearted. He rescues those who are crushed in spirit.' (Psalms 34:18)

In Jeremiah 31:34, we read the promise of the new covenant, 'I will forgive their iniquity, and I will remember their sins no more.' God not only forgives man's sins, but He also forgets them, casts them behind His back, remembering them no more against that man forever. I do not know how He can do it, but He does it because He is God' (Taken from 'The Best of Treasured Gleanings' compiled by JL Tucker). Yes, Jesus casts our sins in the depths of the ocean, (Micah 7:19), so why so we go deep sea diving to retrieve them and carry the guilt? Our God is a forgiving God, and He does forgive and forget all our sins if we confess them to Him and truly repent. (See I John 1:9)

'Christ came to break the shackles of sin-slavery from the soul. 'If the Son, therefore shall make you free, you shall be free indeed.' The Law of the Spirit of life in Christ Jesus 'sets us free' from the law of sin and death.' (Romans 8:2) The only condition of which the freedom of man is possible is that becoming one with Christ. The truth shall make you free (John 8:32) and Christ is the truth.' (Desire of Ages by EG White)

(Taken from Volume 4, Issue 1 from" Freedom Within" 2001)

"One Lord, One Faith, One Baptism"

"May 6, 2001, at the Chapel of the Maine State Prison in Thomaston, I witnessed one of the most beautiful baptisms that I have ever attended. I correspond with, and visited many inmates, but this time I had been invited to witness such a blessed event. I felt so honored that my friend John invited me. I also got to meet three other candidates, Robin, Rod, and Erik.

Many other inmates that were friends of the candidates joined those who were guests singing wonderful praises to the Lord through old familiar hymns. Dean, Mike, and Milton shared their God-given musical and vocal talents with us, and we were truly blessed by their music. Chaplain Matt gave an excellent baptism message and then each candidate gave a moving and heart felt testimony. Erik and Robbin were baptized by Pastor Ed, who ministers to the Lincoln County Jail. John and Rod were baptized by Chaplain Matt. 'Repent and be baptized everyone of you in the name of Jesus Christ… And ye shall receive the gift of the Holy Ghost.' (Acts 2:38)

After the baptisms were finished, we had a chance to have pictures taken and a time of fellowship. It was great to meet some of the inmates that had corresponded with me and to spend time with those that I had met in a more relaxed atmosphere than the visiting room.

It is a blessing to see the Christian community growing at the Maine State Prison and 'Freedom Within' would like to congratulate these brothers in Christ. 'Therefore, if any man be n Christ, he is a new creature: old things are passed away; behold, all things are become new.' (I Corinthians 5:17)

'Being confident of this very thing, that He which hath begun a good work in you will perform it until the day of Jesus Christ.' (Philippians 1:6) Jesus said, 'He who believes and is baptized will be saved' (Mark 16:16. He also told His disciples, 'Go therefore and make disciples of all nations baptizing them in the Name of the Father, the Son and the Holy Spirit.' (Matthew 28:19)...the ties that bind Christians to their heavenly Father and to one another are stronger and truer than even their blood ties and more enduring' (EG White)."

(Taken from Volume 4 Issue 3 of "Freedom Within" 2001)

From left to right: Back row – Pastor Ed, Chaplain Matt, and John

Front Row: Robin, Erik, and Rod

From left to right: Charlotte Fernald, Bible Worker, Sherril Thibodeau of T. Ministries, John (Inmate MSP) and Pauline Nota of "Freedom Within"

"Wake-Up Call"

"I think of 911 emergency 'wake-up call' and the events that led up to that fateful day on 9/11/01, when an unseen enemy attacked our country. It was a horrifying and devastating day, which will never be forgotten. The World Trade Center had been a terrorist target in 1993 and what about the USS Cole? Did we think that if we survived those smaller attacks, which were also 'wake-up calls' that the terrorists would perform their cowardly and evil acts in other countries only? After all we are the most powerful country and the freest in the world and shouldn't they fear us?

As a child I remember praying and reciting the 'Pledge of the Allegiance' to the flag of the United States of America. I remember the Memorial Day parades and people honoring and saluting our flag because it was a symbol of our country, and it represented the sacrifice of all those who fought and shed blood for this country. Freedom came at such a great price. Just as we have taken the sacrifice of Jesus for granted we have taken our freedoms for granted. We have replaced the true heroes who willingly gave their lives for those freedoms with rock stars, movie stars, and people who make a living our of distorting and destroying our need for God. As we continue to throw God out of our schools and country we see our children reap what we have sown. We see shootings in our schools, and there is much rage and raging in our youth. They haven't been taught to respect God and our country, and we will be held accountable for not censoring the trash they view on televsion and pronographic material that is so readily available. When men commit horrific crimes, such as using their planes to destoy more than 6,000 human beings, we wonder why God, who is such a loving God, would allow such a tragedy to occur. Could it be that more than 6,000 people were martyred, resulting in bringing the nation to its knees with many confessing, repenting and finally accepting Jesus as their Savior? He weeps when we grieve, but He created this world and had a right to do with it as He pleases, but He never strikes without warning. 'I will punish the world for evil, and the wicked for their iniquity.' (Isaiah 13:11) God used Noah to warn the people of the impending flood for 120 years because of the wickedness of man (Genesis 6:5-7). Only Noah's family of eight were saved. What about when God sent the prophet Jonah to warn Nineveh? They were repentant and Nineveh was saved. In Genesis chapters 18 and 19 we read about the destruction of the wicked cities of Sodom and Gormorrah, and how

Abraham pleaded with the Lord to save those two cities even for the sake of ten righteous people and the Lord agreed, but only four were righteous and the cities were destroyed by fire. Billy Graham once said 'If God doesn't do something soon, He'll have to apologize to Sodom and Gormorrah, because it is worse now than then.' When the Supreme Court of the United States legalied abortion. Which has resulted in the slaughter of millions of innocent babies, and also legalizing the burning and descreation of our American flag, then I can certainly agree with his statement.

We are very proud Americans and always displayed the American flag, and it is wonderful to see so many more Americans who do believe that God had blessed America abundantly. We grieve for the many who have died for this country and for those and their families who died in the NY, Washington, and PA. We pray that they did not die in vain and that millions will live to worship God and the country He created. We are in the end times and the prophecies in Matthew, Chapter 24 have almost been fulfilled. Christ's second coming has been mentioned 318 times in the New Testament and He tells us in the Bible how to get ready for His coming. As you study the prophecies in Daniel and Revelation, you will also see that what occurred on 9/11/01 is part of those prophecies, but God says that before man destroys this world He will come again.

I pray that we will heed our 'wake-up calls' and that God blesses, unites and heals this nation. Let's be a repentant nation as Nineveh was so we can all be saved. God is still in control and the advice He gives in Joshua 1:9 is sufficient for all God's people. 'Be strong and courageous. Not be terrified; do not be discouraged, for the Lord your God will go with you wherever you go.'" (Taken from Volume 4 issue 4 of "Freedom Within" 2001)

Behind These Walls

This chapter is dedicated to the writings of Robert W. Salo, a former inmate of Maine State Prison.

Gazing into the mirror I see a face staring back at me.
It's not the same one I remember as a child.

CHAPTER THREE

"Reflections in the Mirror"

It is even not the one of a few years ago.
The guilt and pain lines have been erased.
The pity and sorrow has vanished,
In it's place I see the Savior's smile.
The eyes are His as is the mouth
Gazing into the mirror I see.
The face of Christ staring back at me.

"Master Craftsman"

"Picture in your mind for a moment the master craftsman looking through his transit and figuring out just where to lay the first block and just exactly where the corner block will go. With care and precison he lays the first one, followed closely by another and another until the wall is complete. Standing beside it you can't see over it, for its primary purpose is to secure those behind it and to keep those on the outside safe from those living "behind these walls."

If you are on the outside looking in, you will see a cell smaller than most dog kennels, a cell that is 6' wide X 7 ' deep and 9' feet tall, though the amenties vary, the usual is a single cot, mattress, and pillow, a toilet, a sink and a light. If you have the where-with-all to purchase a TV and a stereo, that is allowed, your clothes (Prison issue) are provided for you, unless you can afford to buy your own, then you can have civilian clothes mailed in. These are rules and regulations to follow and corrections fot those not followed.

Picture in your mind for a moment, the Master Craftsman looking through His transit and figuring out just where to lay the first stone for His church, knowing that there are those 'behind these walls' who are ripe for the harvesting, with just a little bit of fertilizer, a whole crop could come from 'behind these walls.' Reverend Matt Kantrowitz is our shepherd, tough, fraught with obstacles at every turn, Matt has managed to turn rotten vessels into ones capable of carrying new wine. Though you always have a few failues, Matt's success rate is pretty high, and I'm sure God is well pleased with him. Matt offers Bible studies 4X per week and a Tuesday night service, a Thursday night Yokefellow service, in addition to our Sunday church service. So you see seeds have been provided, and many souls have been harvested from 'behind these walls,'"

(Taken from Volume 1 Issue 3 of 'Freedom Withn' 1998)

Joyce A. Leonard

"Types of Prisons"

"Greetings the love and peace which our Savior and Christ Jesus has bestowed upon us. 'Remember those in prison as though you were fellow prisoners, and those who are mistreated as if you yourselves were suffering.' (Hebrews 13:3) So many times we tend to forget that there are many types of prisons. Oh yeah, there are no physical bars or walls, but there estraint factor is just as real as mortar and steel fabrications. In real time prisons we have a release date, i.e., parole date to something along those lines. In a physological prison the only release comes in the form of a cure. Man, stubborn creature that we are, more times than not choses to struggle with the idea that he himself can conqueor these problems by himself, only to continue a downward decent into an unfathomable maze.

There is only one choice to select that I know for a fact that it works. I have a phone number for you to call, and it will be the only phone number you will ever need. (Jeremiah 33:3) 'Call to Me and I will answer you, and will tell you great and unsearchable things that you do not know.' This is God's phone number. While serving time in USP Louisburg, PA. I ran across a fellow prisoner who was struggling with a breathing ailment and the fact that he did not know who he was. But…he was searching. And he was the one who showed me God's phone number. Brother Gerald now runs a prison ministry out of Waynesville, NC called 'Jesus Never Fails Ministry,' and he is doing great and wonderful things in Jesus' Name. He also no longer has breathing problems."

'But they that wait upon the Lord shall renew their strength, they shall mount up on wings of eagles, they shall run and not be weary, they shall walk and not faint.' If ever there is a pasage to give one a sense that they could overcome all things, Isaiah 40:31 is it! Many times I would be in the yard exercising and trying to run just one more lap and thought that I could not, but when I started reciting this verse, I found I could and did forge onward.

Sure, we can try all man's remedies and still fall short of the victory celebration, but if we call out to our Lord and Savior Jesus

Christ, we cannot fail, and He will not let us down. You have tried everything else, so why not choose Christ, besides what have you got to lose except your psychological shackles? I for one found out that prison is only in the mind, and with Christ all things are possible. Though I am still *'behind these walls'* I am freer than many I correspond with on the streets.

Many times through our lives, we experience times of insecurity and instability in our life as with you on the other side of these walls, we too only have one answer to depression and that is total immersion in the Word of God, total prayer time, and last but not least, full fellowship with fellow saints, *'behind these walls.'*

(Taken from Volume 1 Issue 4 of 'Freeedom Within' 1998)

"Brotherly or Sisterly Love"

"*Greek* verb Agapao which means ardantly, perfectly (Agape). This is the love we share with God. The Greek verb Phileo, means to like, to be fond of, feel friendship for one another is Philos. Greek Eros love mens of the flesh. Not bad huh? We are given three ways to love in this world, but only two of them are relatively sin free. But the ones I desire to discuss in this 'Behnd These Walls' segmant are of the Agape and Philos type.

Some twenty years ago, my mother and her sister fell apart and have stayed that way even until today. One side says one thing and the other counters with something else. Remember our childhood, back when life was much simpler? Well, back then we used to squabble over little things and bicker back and forth, but after a day or two we made up and that was that, but all in all it was quite childish. Well, that is the way I look at my mother and her sister. They both confess Jesus Christ, but they both still haven't gotten over the imaginary spilt milk.

Recently my mother took the initiative to take the first step toward reconciliation, only to have her face slapped in the form of a restraining order filed for her by her sister. For years my mother bore the brunt of this squabble by being made a parish in her family, always being told she was to blame and if she really was a Christian she would be willing to forgive her sister. Now she knew that was going to take higher intervention if any form of reconcilliation was to be achieved.

First John 2 says in verses 3-5 'And hereby we do know that we know Him, if we keep His commandments. He that saith, I know Him and keepeth not His commandments, is a liar, and the truth is not in him. But whosoever keeps His Word, in him verily the love of God is perfected: hereby know that we that are in Him.' Verse six states, 'He that sayeth that he abideth in Him ought also to walk even as He walked.'

It goes on in verse seven to say, 'Brethren, I write no new commndment unto you, but an old commandment which ye had from the beginning. Again a new commandment I write to you, which thing is true in him and in you; because the darkness is past, and the true light now shineth. He that sayeth he is in the light, and hateth his brother is in darkness even until now. He that loveth his brother shines in the light and there is none occasion of stumbling in him. But he that hateth his brother is in darkness, and walketh in darkness, and knoweth not wither he goeth, because the darkness has blinded his eyes.'

Further on in Chapter three we discover the verses 15-18, 'Whosoever hateth his brother is a murderer, and ye know that no murderer has eternal life. Hereby percieve the love of God, because He laid down His life for us, and we ought to lay down our lives for the brethren. But whoso hath this world's goods, and seeth his brother hath need, and shutteth up his bowels of campassion from him, how dwelleth the love of God in him? My little children, let us not love the world, neither in tongue; but in deed and in truth.'

'Greater is He that isin us than he that is in the world.' (I John 4:4) I seek not to condemn neither my aunt nor my mother, for neither am I without sin, but rather remind them that they too serve a risen Savior, One that requires us as His children to love one another as He loves us, and One who is compassionate and willing to forgive as we ought also to forgive from 'Behind These Walls.'"

(Taken from Volume 1 Issue 5 from "Freedom Within" 1998)

"Media Declaration vs. Defended"

"Judgement? While on the streets, the normal citizen walks through their existence never really realizing just how muuch 'Big Brother' is watching over them, or how much wool is being pulled over their input, or to what degree the candy coating distorts. That is until they come across the thin blue line, and discover that life on the other side is in drastic contrast to their former slow paced life. The rules have changed, where before they were innocent until proven guilty, they now find themselves regarded guilty by everyone, even their loved ones, and mostly because that roving newspaper reporter has deemed them guilty.

News media plays a very large role in securing guilt in today's court room arena. Let's investigate the judgement processs. First your neighbors deem your actions good or bad, innocent or guilty, then the police get their turn followed closely by the inmate population of the recieving facilty, and your attorney then decides just how much effort he or she is going to have to put in to your defense, finally you think it is the judge's turn. Wrong! Now the media gets closer birds eye view to scrutinize your actions before they turn the selction dial over to the jury of your peers. You now have twelve men and women with 12 different sets of opinions whereby they will govern your chances of innocence or guilt. If they slept on the wrong side of the bed or awoke with a splittling headache, these factors weigh heavily into the selection process of their judgement.

Finally after months of wrangling in and out of the court room you are ready to be judged by the judge. If you have been deemed innocent, you are released although you are always deemed 'suspect.' But if you are found guilty, and if you are unfortunate enough to have recieved a lengthy sentence, the judgement process is the beginning, for now you have all the guards at the recieveing facility who judge you anew. Then all the inmates who judge you, and then you are placed in a cell where your new life behind bars begins. Whew! It's finally over. The judgement process ifs finally complete. Wrong again! For every new guard and every new inmate will have to judge anew your life as they see it. Every time a guard shakes down your cell and places contrband in it, you are open to new judgement. It is a vicious cycle of seemingly never ending judgement.

'Behind These Walls' the word rehabilitation takes on a whole new meaning. If you do not rehabilitate yourself then you remanin the same until release, just a few years older. I have found that all the programs offered by the institution have only one thing in common and that is how the statistics look on paper at what they are doing. The only true form of rehabilitation 'behind these walls' is through Christianity. It gives one a chance to review their lives and look for a chance to better themselves in the blood of Christ. They have a chance to shed their old bodies and receive a new one which gives them a hope of eternal rest and their new found Lord and Savior, the Son of the living God.

Ironic, but the judgement process for Christians begin anew. Now your every move is scutinized because now they see you are not falling from man's judgement but from God's. Before if you swore, it was acceptable, but now they see an impersonator, someone who says they are Christian, but their actions say otherwise. You write to a church asking for a assistance and more times than not they judge you. Oh, it is fine that you have selected Christianity, as a way to better your life, but keep it 'behind these walls.' Not all churches see you as different, but many do. And colleges…I have applied to quite a few, but none would accept me, not because I couldn't pay, and not because I desired to advance my learning of Christ, but because I was in jail, though they never seem to look at the Christian, but only what once I had been.

The overview is not coming from a disgruntled inmate, for I break the mold, and am truly guilty of my crimes. I plead guilty. I knew as God did of my guilt. Upon accepting Christ in 1985, I strove to better myself only to be turned away by numerous churches across the U.S. and it wasn't until 1993 that I found a church that saw the Christian and not the criminal and invited me to become part of their congregation from 'behind these walls.' The Augusta Church of Christ accepted me as a brother in Christ, not as a criminal from "behind these walls."

(Taken from Volume 2 Issue 1 from "Freedom Within 1999)

"Which Direction Reflects Jesus?"

Of current events, like all things worth waiting for, they are usually fraught with miscellaneous disappointments and set backs at unthought junctions. Well, my college package wasn't one to let me down on any of these areas. Giving a brief history concerning this adventure takes us back to Leavenworth, KS, in the year 1989. I mailed my first inquiiry to IBC in Florence, Alabama in the early part of 1989. I was told they didn't accept prisoners until they had been out at least a year and had a good conduct record. I was miffed to put it mildly. I was downright mad. What right did they have to reject me and discriminate against me just because of my present place of residence? At that stage I was an infant in Christ, and not accustomed to accepting 'no' answers, much the same as any young child would have.

It put me in a tailspin falling into some pretty depraved things, among them allowing myself to honestly believe that I could do drugs and worship Jesus Christ at the same time. If Christ couldn't even help me to get into a college that prepared people for His ministry, just how powerful was He anyways? I slipped into an abyss just somewhere between barely living and hell. I wasn't a very good listener, for if I had been I wouldn't have heard 'no' but rather 'not now.' But I had my mind made up, I was going to represent Jesus Christ, and I was going to lead others to Christ. The problem was for as much effort I was putting into leading, Satan was putting as much effort into leading me in the opposite direction. This miscalculation in direction went on for almost three years until I was involved in a fight, which you could say brought me to my knees and made me realize I was headed toward a destruction instead of salvation. This transformation was not immediate, for I was still convinced that I could lead both lives with just a bit more moderation and it would all meet up somewhere, up ahead and boy, did it ever meet up ahead!

In 1993, just a few weeks after being returned to the State of Maine from Federal incarceration, I started getting short of breath and feeling light-headed. After practically collapsing I was taken to the hospital and diagnosed with IHSS, a heart defect which I had always known about but never really paid attention to. I was placed on medication which only allowed me to survive easier, but not seem to improve, try as I might this still was not the catalyst which broke the mold of the know-it-all, does it all. I was still too headstrong with my own ideas to see those of Christ.

In 1997, after three and a half years of different medications and numerous episodes of dizziness to palpitations, I finally heard the call loud and clear. 'You have got to change. How long do you expect Me to keep carrying you? This operation could very well decide the outcome of the rest of your life.' Of course this voice was inside my head, as it had been most of my life, but this time I knew it was more than a rash moment of hearing voices...but Jesus was speaking personally to me as He always had. I am not perfect by any standards, but I smoked my last joint in 1995, and I took my last acid trip back in 1992. I still have weaknesses, as does most anyone. I know who believes in Christ, but now I curb the impulses better and strive to make the bad areas in my life dissapate with His assisstance.

The operation was successful and I've more or less returned to normal, of course I am still medicated, but it actually works now. After all this time, I finally found out I'd been accepted as a distance learning student through IBC. They mailed my books to the wrong address, but God's hand was on this transaction because they accepted them here at the prison even through all these misadventures. I started college on Monday, with new appreciation of Jesus' love for me and with more to look forward to than what I had in the hind side of my life."

(Taken from Volume 2 Issue 2 of "Freedom Within" 1999)

"A Karios Experience"

From 'behind these walls' LOVE is watching a group of diversely different men meeting from the outside with one goal in mind, and that is searching for their individuality, their own sense of spirituality, and discovering their source of anger. Love is watching these same group of men from 'behind these walls' look at each other with contempt, scorn, fear and a sense of distrust, in the first three hours in their four day journey before it comes to an end, and they have come face to face with their demons, and the face of Christ seperated by a gulf of love, of which they do not understand. 'Behind these walls' the second day begins with hugs and handshakes. The distrust is still reveling like a cold north wind blowing across a northern Maine town, but for those men who have opted to quit are starting to melt just slightly, perhaps with a gentle smile, or a careleess shrug of their shoulders, a nervous twitch of the eye, or perhaps they are just starting to pay attention, but whatever the sign, day two has begun. The first hour is taken up by fellowship and getting reaquainted, eating treats which is foreign to the residents 'behind these walls,' and gentle nudges toward the cross of Jesus. There are talks and discussions throughout the day, there are admissions of hate and guilt, there are a couple of home cooked meals prepared out of love from the area churches. There are alot of encouragment and a few tears and day two is over.

'Behind these walls' the start of day three signals, a sort of dysfunctional melt down. Fears have started to fade. Anger has been tempered. Walls and barriers are starting to crumble and the love of Jesus is starting trickle in between the cracks of their exterior forming a new found experience known as the Christian experience. The letting go of pride and the molding of a new life. We start the third day, the same way as the first two, with the exception of those men who had shrunk from mere touchng of human bonding were now accepting gentle hugs and handshakes. They were experiencing the LOVE of the unadulterated kind and feeling the Spirit of Jesus ooze over their souls for perhaps the first time and it is not scaring them anymore. There were more experinces of their shared past, hatred of times of distrust, and a break down of barriers which had allowed Satan to influence their lives since birth. The sharing and the tears were flowing more freely and a sense of comradship was forming. Brothers in Christ were being born.

'Behind these walls,' the final day was upon us, and no one, not even the most ardent, stubborn person could believe it was almost over, and they had withstood three days of intense indocrination into Christian attitudes and the breakdown of self. The day started much more jovial than the preceeding three. The ice that thwarted the journey up the island lake where their most precious and stubbornly released frustration was bottled up and not thawed entirely for there was still a little more work to be performed to melt that final ice cube blocking Christs' way. It is hard to believe what a small slip of paper can hold when used for the good of mankind and the spread of Christianity when a piece of paper just six inches in length and one-half inch wide melted the last ice cube and allowed the flow of LOVE to encapsulate an entire room catapulting them into a new found life, with a new Master and Savior, Jesus Christ.

'Behind these walls,' Love is seeing that one last ice cube melt and the flood of anguish and hatred cascade out through the reservoir to be replaced with LOVE and freedom that only the Savior can order. While watching that last individual our of twenty-three men to acccept a hug for the first time of pure agape LOVE and not shirk in disdain as a new brother shares in his new experience, a Christian walk, 'Behind these Walls.'"

(Taken from Volume 2 Issue 3 of "Freedom Within" 1999)

"Too Long Seperated from Him"

"*Stuck*...within a world...a place where love is but a memory... almost a fleeting glimpse of past occurances...stalked by hatred, the identificcation code for the deceivers...tears form seperating guilt for some crashing those of others...pathetic whiners deceiving themselves into thinking darkness is light...that the fire that is scorching their souls is really a cool breeze soothing...almost at the brink of total deception, a glimmer of hope filters in through a portal which streams through just a mere trickle of Christ's love.

The beast within tries to hide but it is found out...his deception, his once gentle voice has turned into a roar of indignation. He has created a rift between the believers...a chasm of doubt, he has caused division within the ranks. He cause total love to part and to be replaced with a partial coverage...an unacceptable medium, when the cup was full, miraculous healings were norm...but seperation has caused the cup to empty, tilting our very existence. Without a full cup, Satan keeps his foot in the door jam. Wake up to the stench of death and destruction. Put an end to the deception and allow the cup to overflow…replacing total deception with total love…hard to believe that hardened criminals sould possibly, for even the wildest stretch of the imagination, be capable of loving anyone else, much less care about anyone other than themselves. But 'behind these walls' a revival of the Maine State Prison, a revival has been occurring and Jesus has been making in roads into a one time honored pit of decadence, a hole where even guards hated to come.

Can tabs were saved by the thousands to be donated to the Shriner's club for dialysis for children, but the powers, 'behind these walls' has deemed this task inappropriate and it no longer occurs. But we still have prayer, and 'fervent effectual prayer of a righteous man availeth much.' 'Confess your faults one to another, and pray for one another, that ye may be healed.' (James 5:16) Though a block has been thrown into our path from one direction, we stepped over it and proceeded toward the light. I don't know how many places on the mean streets of America, where the average citizen can go each and every day to find prayer meetings and Bible studies everyday of the week, but here, 'behind these walls' we can! On Sunday we have an average of two monthly concerts from outside churches. We have Karios Prison Ministry, which holds seminars for new members twice a year and holds meetings here, 'behind these walls.' I can personally attest to growth 'behind these walls,' as I have witnessed transformations of men who for years were so bitter you didn't want to have anything to do with them, but now you desire their company and to hear what Jesus is doing in their lives. I guess you can deduce from everything I have been saying, that the common denominator here is: 'Jesus Christ and His eternal love.' For too long we have been seperated from 100% of His LOVE by your own actions and deeds, we have allowed His gift to weaken our denominationalism. We have been concerned with how we can change the world and forgotten that unless what we do is filtered through Christ's LOVE we can do nothing of ourselves. We need unity of our faiths. Do we not all serve a risen Savior, Jesus Christ? Then lets all serve Him as one body and not many splits of the vine which leads to His LOVE, one limb, one body, the body of Christ."

(Taken from Volume 2 Issue 4 from "Freedom Within: 1999)

"New Beginnings"

"*I beseech* you therefore, brethren, by the mercies of God, that ye present your bodies a living sacrifice, holy acceptable unto God, which is your reasonable service. And be not conformed to the world but be ye transformed by renewing of your mind, what is good, and acceptable, and perfect will of God." (Romans 12:1-2)

"Let's tear these two verses apart and look deeper into what they are saying, by going to the Greek text, and the Hebrew. 'Beseech' in the Greek-*parakateo* to call aside, make an appeal in view of certain facts. Here is an appeal in view of the wonderful doctrines of Romans chapters 1-8 and all of God's dispensational dealings with Jews and Gentiles in chapters 9-11. Paul comes now to the pracical application of the gospel to men (12:1 -15). Our next word is 'mercies' in the Greek – *oiktirmos*, tender, compassions used in 2 Corinthians 1:3; Phillipains 2:1; Colossians 3:12; Hebrews 10:28, and Matthew 9:16. 'Present' meaning men are now to bring themselves to God instead of sacrifices to the altar of the the old. They are now to be wholly the Lord's as were the former sacrifices.

"Reasonable,' which means radical worship, being performed with the heart, mind and soul of intelligent human beings and is now contrast to the worshp of idols of Romans 1:25. In the second verse we find two commands beginning with the word 'conformed' from the Greek *suschematizo*, to conform to another example. This is used in the verse and also in I Peter 1:14. The word 'world' from the Greek – *aion* meaning age. Paul is saying, do not pattern after this age or to the times. This is also found in Hebrews 1:2. Next 'tansformed,' from the Greek – *metamorpheoo*, transformed or transfigured by supernatural change, as in Matthew 17:2, Mark 9:22, Romans 12:2, II Corinthinas 4:16, Colossians 3:10, Hebrews 6:6, and Ephesians

4:23. Conclusion: There are six things that constitute the acceptable and perfct will of God (Romans 12:2).

1. Present your bodies a living sacrifice to God (Romans 12:2).
2. Make the body holy (Romans 12:1. II Corinthinas 2:1).
3. Make self acceptble to God (Romans 12:1).
4. Render reasonable service (Romans 12:1).
5. Be not conformed to the world (Romans 12:2).
6. Be transformed from the world (Romans 12:2).

This brings us to 'perfect' from the Greek – *teleios* meaning that which has reached its end; nothing more to complete it. Pretty heavy two little verses when you tear them apart and try to deceipher their actual meaning as they were intended to be read. So as we end our century and get ready to begin a new one, we pass from one year into another, finding very unique situation from which to view our past and our future.

In the past our lives may not have been acceptable unto God, even though we have been baptized but now we can have a future that is acceptable to Him. We can give it all to God, both out here in the mean streeets of America and 'behind these walls.'"

(Taken from Volume 3 Issue 1 from "Freedom Within" 2000)

"Fellowship"

"Imagine for a brief moment, that you have had the most spectacular event ever happen to you in your short life here on earth and the ending result was to be ordered to serve 50 years in prison. Imagine still, that you have always known right from wrong, yet still due to the mental defect, you still slipped further from grace than you had ever planned. This scenerio is not so far fetched for it happened to me in the month of June 1978.

Since we are just imagining, let us imagine further that while you are incarcerated, you develop a relationship with a few individuals and they all belong to the same church, and after a few short months, the same people allow you to become a member, from 'behind these bars.' Life is sweet. How much better can life get? Sure you are still behind bars, but you have people that undersatnd you, and accept you as how you are now, and not how you used to be. Many nights I sit in my cell at the Maine State Prison, and wonder how my new found brothers and sisters are doing.

Are they nice people? Of course they must be! But I have never met the majority of them, so this is all idle speculation. I also got to wonder what they think of me and wonder what their idle speculation merits them? Don't get me wrong now, I am not complaining about the few individuals from the church that I have actually met. I realize the fear of getting too close to an incarcerted person, and I understand you have other people more important in your life.

I hope I don't blow any minds here with the next statement, but I have been gazing into the past way before I was born, at events that occurred around my Savior's birth, of His growing up years, 'cause let's face it, Christ was as human as you and I while He was here on the earth with us. There was probably many moments in His earthly life when He desired companionship more than anything else in the world. I believe He achieved His best when He went off in the wilderness. He found an opportunity to be around other celestial beings, i.e. angels, His Father, for man could not have been able to accept the encounters with things they might not understand, but of course you must attribute this to all the idle speculation from 'behind these walls' for I have no scripture to back up these ideas, but I know if I myself needed companionships, or fellowship, then the Master of whom I am shaped in His image must also have had similar needs. Now here is the big question. Let's forget about myself for a minute – how many out there in the world utilize to the utmost of their accessibility to fellowship with other church members? Do you visit those who cannot participate due to physical limitations? Do you embrace your brother and sister's problems as your own or do you only concern yourself with those issues that pertain basically to your own family? Christ gave us an example by entertaining us with exerpts from His life, His denominations on how we should act, and

He came down here to earth not to prove that He can become a man b ut that He was. I cannot fellowship with the brothers and sisters of faith from 'behind these walls' personally but I can and do so in spirit and ink.

(Taken from Volume 3 Issue 2 from "Freedom Within" 2000)

"Christ at The Helm"

"*Ever* look out at the water and look at the boat that never seemed to go anywhere? Or perhaps it goes somewhere, but it just doesn't go in a straight course. Perhaps there are no oars, or maybe there isn't a rudder, without some way to steer the boat, it seems to go wherever the tide takes it or where the wind blows. Now look at that man, he's got two feet, and a naviagational center in his shoulders. Yet, if he does not have a rudder, he will go round in circles just like the boat. Oh, it might be more complex then the boat, but none the less, a man without a direction is like a boat without a rudder.

There are many rudders yet to be found in this world, ones that take you to oblivion, ones that give you that get-rich feeling, ones that stay in the same place never going more than a few miles in any direction, and then there is the Bible, the Word of God. Now here is a rudder that has been places. And we all know what happens to a rudder if it is not well maintained. It falls into disrepair and it falls by the way side. The same thing happens when we fail to maintain our Bible reading. That really great experience when we find Jesus is standing right beside us, holding our head above the waters of uncertainty. The exhilerating high that no drug can match. We loose all this when we fail to maintain the proper repair in our life that only the Bible can bring.

You can tell me, 'Bob, I never had that problem.' But I can tell you that you have. I don't know anyone around who hasn't had this at least once in their lifetime. It is not a forced experience. It it was the only thing that could keep that battery in our car running, you would read it everyday in order to keep commuting. But it is the only thing that will keep your life running throughout eternity. So why don't we take out a little insurance policy and take the time to read it each and every day.

We now have a rudder, so we can go in any direction that it leads, so now we have to find a helmsman, someone to steer this so called boat. It can't be just anyone, because we know what kind of mess we have made with our own lives. If we go to our rudder, and ask it what we should do, it tells of a Helmsman like no other, tall, true, kind, compassionate, and one that all you men can look up to; one that would be willing to give His own life for you. Jesus Christ will be my Helmsman.

Now I got my rudder and someone to steer my boat, and even a direction in which to head for, now all I need is a compass. That way I will never get lost. What? You say the Helmsman already has a compass, then I guess I have no reason but to always be on course. Strange how looking at an idle boat floating upon the water can present such a startling discovery, but one last observance has to be made. How do I keep in contact with my Helmsman while I am being held 'behind these walls?' An intercom would work quite nicely, but since I don't have one, the rudder says I should pray. Praying is as important as reading the Bible, for one compliments the other. So now I have a Rudder, a Helmsman, a Compass, and an Intercom for direct comversation. I am ready to start my journey. How about you?"

(Taken from Volume 3 Issue 3 from "Freedom Within" 2000)

"The Perfect Friend"

"*Ever* had a friend...one that could do no wrong? One that you just had to seek his approval before you did something on your own? One that if they said 'yes' everything would turn out right? Perhaps it was an elder brother or sister, or perhaps it was your mom or dad, but there was definitely someone whom you looked up to and sought their acceptance or permission before you acted upon your impulse. The same should be true in our spiritual lives. We should always seek out the wisdom of the Master. And how do we do this? We do it through prayer. Just like our earthly fathers, our heavenly Father desires our requests, and petitions for His guidance. He wants us to seek His approval.

Instead, now that we are much older, we no longer feel the compulsion to seek out other's wisdom, for now we are the ones in control, we hold the big spoon. We wear the big shoes. We can do anything we desire. We can drink as late as we want, we can stay out all night till the cows come home, we can swear, in fact, the sky is the limit to what we can do, now we are in charge. Hey! What is this? As I open the large envelope and examine the electric bill for $65, and then the one for the water for $45, and they just seem to go on forever. You begin to wonder if you have any money left from your $200 paycheck to do any of the things that you love to do so much. I guess we have to rethink a few priorities or go out and find another job. 'Whoa, Bob! That was a red light we just went through! Ah, don't worry about it, Sam, we were the only ones there. No one got caught, there ain't nothin' to worry about!' Or, 'Hey Bob, you just broke that plate glass window! We better run or we'll get caught. Yea, I guess we better.' The list goes on and on about the things we do and seem to get away with, but let me tell you the meter is running and every transgression is a deed being recorded in a book that will not get lost, or burnd in a fire, in fact, this book will last for an eternity. We can get these things erased but we have to go to the Father. Our Father in heaven, for He is the One Who knew we would do this before we did and He also knew He would give us good counsel, if we would just ask Him.

In the Book of Romans, in the seventh chapter, there is a section that deals wirh the things of life that we should do. I know in my life, I just had to press the envelope as far as physically possible. Stopping short of death in my own frivolous attempt at doing whatever and how often I wanted to do that and should not, but yet I did. I smoked dope, did LSD, more than most individuals who still have their sanity intact. Overdose after overdose, attempt at sucide, being in accidents that should have killed me, but did not even injure me. All this occurred before my last and extremely final fall from grace, and I still have not learned my lesson.

In 1978, the month of June, I decided to let God have enough fun and decided I would become God (if only in my mind). I decided to take another life, to make a long story short, I ended up in prison for a period of 50 earthly years. I guess my stint of being God didn't quite pan out. In fact anything I felt that I myself could achieve, turned out quite badly. Even inside I refused to heed the call of Jesus, and I continued to do drugs, maim others, and go diving downward toward the very pits of despair, until 1985. I finally met the Man I sought all my life. One that I could have met on the outside, but had to fall so far and then meet Him in prison, Jesus Christ. From that day on, my liife drastically changed. Oh it hasn't been a bed of roses. I was not immediately released from prison, for He never promised that, but rather He offered me a lifestyle that would one day culminate with eternal life with Him in heaven. So even after doing all this time behind bars, I can still look forward to eternal life from 'behind these walls,' with Jesus Christ. Just ask His approval today and he will set you free."

(Taken from Volume 3 Issue 4 from "Freedom Within' 2000)

"Revival"

"Greetings in the name of Jesus! How many times have you been out on the road and seen one of those huge tents erected beside the road with large banners proclaiming that there was a 'Revival' inside tonight? Did you snicker or make some obnoxious joke about it and just continue on your way? Later on did you wonder what might have taken place behind the flaps of that huge tent? Did you imagine that some secretive society was holding dark and hidden ceremonies just out of the sight of the rest of the world? Well, I know I did, as the Spirit will often do when we least expect it. I went in behind the enomous flaps of that huge and formidable tent and discovered just what Jesus had planned for me.

As I walked inside, I was met by a group of extremely nice people. They welcomed me and told me that Jesus loved me, and they showed me to my seat. Now I want to tell you that up until that moment, I had been truly amazed to find really nice people inside that tent, but as our minds will often do from time to time, I just figured this was part of the grander and more elaborate scheme just waiting to be sprung. At precisely 9:00 PM the enormous tent flaps were closed, and a man dressed entirely in black walked from the back up to the pulpit. He just stood there for a few minutes looking around the huge tent, almost as if he were sizing up the crowd he was preparing to fleece, waiting for exactly the right moment to pounce. Boy, I was in for a shock, for neither did I expect, nor do I think that anyone else did, when he opened his mouth to speak, his words were like music to the ears.

He asked for a show of hands for all of those who truly knew the Lord. After that he asked all those who raised their hands to assist him in helping those who had not raised their hands in preparation of this revival service and helping them feel more comfortable in their presence. So, we turned to each other and either hugged or shook hands. The love in that room was so thick you could have cut it with a knife. He next started to preach. He talked about God and how He made the earth in six days and on the 7th day He rested. He talked about Noah and the Flood, of Abraham and Isaac, about David and Solomon and about Job and Jonah and about Jesus and John. In the course of a few short minutes, we had gone from Genesis to John. Every eye was focused on the front and every ear was strained on the man up front all dressed in black in fear that they would not see something or hear something.

When he looked your way, it was if you were the only one in the room and as if his questions were directed toward you. When he made an accusation, it was also only directed at you. If you could have been in the bodies of the other revivalists, you would have realized that everyone in that huge tent was thinking the same thoughts, that this guy truly cared for each and every one of them. He had an altar call and invited many to come up front, as, many as was desirous to receive the gift offered exclusively by Jesus Christ as a special dispensation from His Father in heaven one that through the blood that was shed up on the cross of Calvary. No matter where you looked, he seemed to be there, administering to all who wanted to receive the gift. I had arrived expecting to lose my shirt and instead I had been offered an opportunity to live forever in paradise. So, the next time you have been feeling that everyone is talking directly to you, maybe they are. Who knows what the Spirit has in store for you today, 'behind these walls.'"

(Taken from Volume 4 Issue 1 from "Freedom Within" 2001)

"Prison Life"

"*Ever* wonder what it would be like to be in prison? Ever wonder what goes through the minds of those incarcerated inmates as they reside behind concrete walls, separated from their loved ones and their friends? Alienation from the planet you were born on, your whole demeanor is altered. The first second after the door slams shut behind you, as you are led hand-cuffed and shackled into a foreign environment, is the longest second of the rest of your life.

If you possess any survival instincts, they immediately kick in, you become wary of everyone. You don't know anyone, and you don't know who you can trust, but there is no way of getting around those steel and concrete barriers so you muckle under and make the best of a bad situation. Every little noise jump starts your senses, your threat security comes measures come online, protectively, subjecting every new encounter as if it were a real thing. The first night in stir could possibly become the longest night of your life. Morning arrives of the first day of your actual sentence 'behind these walls' and you greet it with some sort of amazement, wondering what your new lifestyle entails. Breakfast was like walking through a minefield, every step measured to ensure proper alignment to the program. The food, probably calling it food is a little too much, but it gets better after a while, but for now it is downright rank. After chow, you are assigned a job, which is necessary to obtain 'good time.' After what seems like an eternity, after you have eaten twice more, you are signaled to go back to your cell and remain there until the next day repeats itself.

You have probably written 20 letters since you have arrived, to everyone starting with mom and ending with your best friend, Tom. As the guard stops in front of your cell, with delight he is holding a handful of letters for you, as you expectantly receive the letters you notice the first one is a 'return to sender' from Suzy, the next one is from Tom, and you discover that each and everyone of your letters have been returned to you, and you realize this new life had a whole new set of rules, the ones that only reply 'behind these walls.' Out of the 20 letters, 19 of them are 'return to sender.' Mom still found a small place in her heart for you and answered your letter.

The scenarios are typical of the incarcerated inmates. Not only are you put on trial, but your family and friends are also put on trial. The likelihood of any of your old friends staying loyal for fear of being ostracized leaves your actual correspondence and limiting lists quite small. I have found a way to bolster correspondence lists by sending them with newfound Christian friends. The hardest problem with this route is ever finding the new friend willing to take the chance to really get to know you. Of course, I have heard of the horror stories where certain inmates are only interested in either fleecing or getting over on their new friends, but that is only about 1.5% of the actual population as there is an inordinate amount of honest and truly relation seeking inmates in here. Many have been in over a decade and never had a visit or a letter. Perhaps one of those individuals who could truly benefit a new relationship with someone from 'behind these walls.'" (Taken from Volume 4 Issue 2 from "Freedom Within" 2001)

"Human Instincts"

WILLFUL, wantonly, desiring beyond measure, we follow a trail through the wilderness of the mind, earnestly searching for the slightest morsel of sanity in the far-reaching madness called reality. The animal kills for food or protection of his family, but the human animal seems to be in turmoil, havoc creating it only set of laws and orders, and religious leaders kill in the name of God, while others use excuses of territorial rights and compressed ideological ideals, which basically seeks to justify their actions gone awry.

Being an ardent believer in the Bible, this present stage, which is set within the world, does not surprise me, in fact this book foretells of the very behavior, where man has run amok further than ever before they explode, the surprise that will beat all surprises will occur and the madness, which is tearing the very fabric of sanity apart will be stopped with a loud trumpeting blare, and I believe that I am going to be there, as the world bucks and pushes in its final throes of vomiting out all those who disrespect. and blatant disregarders of mother nature's golden rule, of using the land and restoring its beauty and sanity before you move to another moment of time.

Cries foul, an eagle sheds tear, which in turn waters a flower, which is gagging on air tainted with pollutants to numerous to list and as the bee skips his stop in it forging for nectar, that's not tainted by man's encroachment, upon its sterile environment; tears now dried, the eagle spirals downward until it flows into the shallow grave within the confines of a brook, where no fish live in nor support any life of any kind, as it ushers forth its last breath, it thinks of a meadow of freshly mowed hay, children romping, laughing and playing without a care in the world; a sky so blue, it hurts your eyes to stare at it for long, and a cool breeze that overshadows the faint scent of daffodils, within of a world without cars and airplanes polluting the air of its mother.

Bitter-sweet fond memories often cloud the mind as confusion laden with tears fog the thin line separating rational thought with implications of massive hysteria, exploding land mines within the brain triggering events beyond the comprehension of rational thoughts. If acted upon this would create the boundaries between sanity and insanity, which cries foul the wandering vagabond who instills his macabre nightmare upon innocent public creating havoc. The extremes of unmentionable acts, created by screams of torment shatters one's sense of solitude ripping the veil of reality, the inner mind reveals a defect within the program, reeling from uncertainty to the command processing the unit shuts down while protecting the soul from vicious intrusions beyond comprehension. As pain engulfs the thoughts and insanity grip the moment, with a fleeting glimpse into the side-stepping criminal mind that unfolds while encapsulating all the fears and preconceptions of all knowledge concerning the infesting parasite known as evil. The twisting fibers of reality, taunt, creating a void between the real and the unreal, a chasm between good and bad, a representative of being called human, as I write from 'behind these walls.'"

(Taken from Volume 4 issue 3 from "Freedom Within" 2001)

"A Dream or Reality"

"*Trudging* along a long dusty, winding path muttering softly to myself as to which way is best, to go to the East or to the West, over and over until it blotted out the high blinding afternoon sun. The screech of severe pain echoes endlessly reverberating between the surrounding mountains using them as a synthetic tympanic membrane telling the world its macabre story, inside my head, it is crawling around inside my head, and it is driving me mad. It is ripping the fabric of reality into shreds. I kept telling myself it was only a dream, and it wasn't making any difference, just this insane urge to mutter, 'go East, go West, which way is best.'

The thumping of a big bass drum awakens me from my fitful slumber. A noise so loud it must have awakened the neighbors, but no, it was only the beating of my heart, thumping so urgently that its message was bypassing the pump and going directly into my ear. The tightness in my chest was so extreme it made me grab it in hopes of manually stopping its urgent throbbing. In the older generation it would have been identified as a nitro moment, but not for someone as young as I. What had gone so tragically wrong, why was the edges of reality so jagged? Why didn't my mom come rushing to give me succor to my extreme behavior, clutching my chest carefully I got up on one side of the bed and stared intently out between the long slender pieces of steel, when it hit me really, really hard that I wasn't in Kansas anymore. I was doing another night in stir. I was riding the sacred steel plate; I was trapped in a world of suspended animation.

Although I may have been a little extreme with my dramatization, I am sure there are many of you who can relate to where I am coming from. The extreme moments are not appearing as often as they used to, which I can attribute to my acceptance of the rules and regulations of the Lord's house in accepting His guarantee of unconditional

Joyce A. Leonard

LOVE and His promise to never leave me. Do you know any mere humans who can back up the same claim and actually pay in advance for your life, paid in full of his own blood? He says, 'pick up your cross and follow Me,' but I have to tell you, brothers and sisters, that is a tall order to follow, but I try as best I can. I believe I can best serve this purpose by trying each day to strive each day by coming one step closer to the cross. I am far from perfect, but He tells us not to worry about this, just trust Him and He will deliver us from all our problems. Nothing is too big for Jesus.

You claim that you cannot do anything to fulfil His call to become a disciple and missionaries, but if all you can do is make a friend who is having a bad day feel a littler better, you have started to do that which Jesus wants us all to do. Feeling that I have the gift of gab, I find myself writing to others, both in two publications as well as in my own feeble attempt at the ministry in the form of the Prayer Warriors for Christ newsletter. I can't toot my own horn and say it is a whopping success, but we have gone from 3 copies to 250 in eight years. So, you can see even a miscreant, such as I, can make a small effort that might be what someone else needs to make their life a little better, even doing this from 'behind these walls.'"

(Taken from Volume 5 Issue 1 from "Freedom Within" 2002)

Robert W. Salo was an inmate at Maine State Prison. He found Jesus Christ "behind these walls" and served Him from there in articles and letters to others. He was born June 2, 1955, and died a free man six months after being released May 2015 after 25 years incarcerated. He had formerly been in the military and served in the US Navy as well as in the US Air Force. He was a member of the Augusta Church of Christ and was active in the missions' program, particularly the outreach through the church to Ethiopia.

Bob was active in the craft room at the prison. He was gifted with creating intarsias.

| Robert Salo in the craft room at Maine State Prison displaying the intarsia of the Last Supper | Intarsia created by Robert Salo especially for the Auburn Seventh-day Adventist Church |

Prisoner's of Hope

This chapter is dedicated to inmates from various prisons that have sent in their thoughts, poetry and drawings complied and selected from the many submissions of the prison newsletter,

"Freedom Within."

Dennis Lennon

CHAPTER FOUR

"Thoughts in the Night"
By Kevin Tardiff – MSP 1998

"While lying here in my cell tonight,
Unable to sleep, my mind in flight
I review my memories of the past,
And wonder why time goes by so fast.
I think of the days when I was a child,
Just a care free kid out running wild;
My thoughts of the future are often shattered,
By things of the present that didn't even matter.
As I grew older, my ways were the same.
I held the twisted idea that life was only a game;
So, to win, I cheated, but instead I lost,
And as a loser, I am paying the cost.
But I ponder these thoughts in the night,
And begin to see my past was not right;
I plan for a future that hope will be
A way of life that will keep me free!"

"TESTIMONY OF TONY ABREAU"

"Born April 1, 1970 in Bronx, NY, raised in Maine and moved around a lot. I spent several years of my life in various locations in South FL I also lived in Alabama and Cleveland, OH briefly. I was abused and the abuser of sexual sins. I was a drug addict and alcoholic. I have probably commited murder, God only knows. Ever since I was eleven years of age I have been in and out of trouble, from detentions to drug programs and group homes to mental institutions, juvenille prisons and finally the adult system.

My earthly father went to prison the day after I was born and was not really a part of my life until he got out 17 years later, only to be murdered two and a half years later. My mother, who at my birth was twenty years of age, and had three children prior to me. She was unstable due in part to drugs, but ultimately she was just in bondage to Satan. Mom couldn't take care of herself and me very well, so she left the Bronx, and came back to her native homeland of beautiful Maine, where her parents, my loving Nana and Grampy, who are still alive (1998) 'Praise God!' long with my Nana Teeney.

Anyway...the Lord provided shelter and shuffling of my life began, I have lived with my grandparents, aunts, uncles and cousins and from time to time in short confusing intervals with friends of the family. Ever since I can remember, I was a trouble maker of some sort or another in school. I recall how I was either the class clown or the bully, sometimes both and other times I was an idiot dunce butt of the peers snide antics, the jock, the burn out, the winner, the loser, the friend to everyone and more often than not the real nowhere man. I grew up real fast and became real street wise, though I was never well at vocalizing all the mixed emotions and hidden fears, trying to meet some sort of lasting peace and stability. I would run away and wander the streets of Miami or wherever and waste away in the ever increasing cesspool of sin and wickedness.

But even though in all this I believd in God and always felt Him watching over me. Still I know I was a disgrace to Him and how I deserved very much to go to Hell. In 1991, I brutally raped a woman. I totally violated and unmercifully and disgraced an innocent old lady. I certainly ought to go to hell now. It was like I was on a life destroy mission and this was the most disgraceful way I could think of...and so I turned myself in and pleaded guilty receiving a twenty year sentence.

Prior to being sentenced, I had eight months in county jail to reflect on the shameful crime I had committed. I was strangely somewhat at peace, due in part, I believe, in the absence of drugs and alcohol, but mostly because I asked God to forgive me, and I just knew He did, and yet there was something eating away at my soul. You see, even though I could feel and comprhend God's forgiveness, I could not forgive myself. And so the pain and misery continued and grew stronger and my self esteem was at an all time low.

I arrived here at the Maine State Prison, 'Tommy Town' as it is unaffectionally sir-named, on June 5, 1992. And the cycle began to roll again, same as it always had before, getting into stupid trouble, trying to fit in and be cool, doing drugs and thinking I was the tough guy, etc., etc. Well, I ended up going to super max prison in Warren and I said to myself, 'Self, you have reached a new plateau in in your stage of abnormal development' and I said to the policeman, 'Hey there Mr. Blue Meanie, can I have one of them there Bibles?' Well sure enough I got one and commenced to reading one of the blessed blessings. Yep, I told the Man I got into this commotion with that landing me here, that I sure was sorry and that I was going to be a Christian again.

There was still a bit of house cleaning to do cause I had not really repented. I wanted to and I said so, but I was still hanging on to the reading material like 'No One Gets Out Alive' the Jim Morrison story and other books such as Jackie Collins and the John Bullushi story. So, I got to the point of privlege where I was allowed to have a TV, and I began to watch the same old crap and my Bible began to collect dust. So, I went for a month or so and got into trouble again, another stupid act of violence. I lost all my privleges and back to basics, just little ole' me and my Bible – praise God!

Well, the good Lord and I had a nice long talk and He let me know that I had to repent and so FINALLY that is what I did. And then I **distinctly** heard Him say to me, 'My son, I want you to praise Me.' Hallelujah! Praise the Lord and Savior Jesus Christ. The Lord used me to set Super Max on fire with His Word the Lord saved me, forgave me, and I have forgiven myself cause it was revealed to me like 'Hey kid, who are you not to forgive yourself, when I have forgiven you.' Today I am a born again Christian.

Oh, I am learning to count the cost and to pick up my cross everyday. I am certainly not perfect, and will never be, but today by God's grace, I am striving to reach the goal of perfection by pursuing righteousness, peace, love and all the fruits of the Spirit. The responsibility and honor of being a Christian is a relationship that I hope I will be faithful until the Lord returns- God bless you in Jesus Name, your brother (in faith) Tony. Shalom"

> "Now the God of peace, that brought again from the dead our Lord Jesus, the great Shepherd of the sheep, through the blood of the everlasting covenant, making you complete in every good work to do His will, working in you that which is well pleasng in His sight, through Jesus Christ; to Whom be glory forever and ever." (Hebrews 13:20-21) Amen.

"Testimony of Jimmy Wood"

"I have lived in a home that was run by abusive alcoholic, and have known the pain that comes from such a way of life. As I grew up, I too became a hopeless drunk, well, hopeless as far as being able to help myself, but after years of drug and alcohol abuse, and many years behind bars, Jesus came to me and set me free. The world will tell you there is no hope for the alcoholic, but the Bible says that Jesus Christ, our only hope and way to eternal life (Romans 10: 9, 10, 13). I have known forgiveness and the joy of salvation, but to my regret, I have backslidden back in 1997. What a painful experience that was, but thanks to God, I was awakened from my spiritual sleep and made my way back home.

If you have backslidden, repent and ask God to forgive you (I John 1:9). Since my return in faith, God has given me a wonderful wife, who has been such a blessing to my life. I am so undeserving, but in spite of that, God continues to use me. Starting over has proven difficult at times, but through Christ all things are possible. (Mark 9:23; Pilippians 4:13). Becoming a Christian behind prison bars was not an easy thing to do, whereas the rest of those I had to live with continued to walk in darkness, God, however, never left my side.

He has given me courage to do His work among a people for the most part, did not want to hear what I had to say. The change that had taken place in me was as obvious as day and night. In spite of that, they refused to let Jesus in. I have a burden on my heart for those in prsion. In a similar way that Paul carried a burden on his heart for the people of Israel.

When I fell back in 1997, I gave in to the cravings of the flesh, which left my mind stained with unforgettable filth so when I did return to the faith, a renewing of the mind was necessary. This renewing process takes place by a daily reading of the Scripture. (Roamsn 12:1-2) 'The Lord knows how to deliver the godly out of temptation.'(2 Peter 2:9) I spent a large part of my life behind priosn walls. Becoming a Christian in prison has given me a deeper insight concerning the need of reaching those men. They live and think just as I once did, but by the grace of God, I have been restored to the faith, for God does not desire that any should perish but to have eternal life." (2 Peter 3:9)

"Hello God"

"Hello God, yes it has been a long time.
Who" Oh momma, she is fine.
Yes, I would like to go for a walk.
I just watched the news last night.
I had to close my eyes real tight.
God, there are three kids killed in Maine,
And a group of homeless sleeping in the rain.
A man from Texas set freee after beating his wife;
A 14 year old boy in Florida took his own life.
'My son, I can see your hurt and concern,
Though there are many lessons to be learned.
I can't stop all this suffering and pain,
For that is a link in life's long chain.'
God, when will all the wars cease?
Is there ever going to be any peace?
'My son, I know it is hard to understand,
The decisions and actions of man.
My child all I can say is pray,
And patiently wait for My return one day.'"

By Jerry Larrivee MSP 1998

Crafted and built by Jerry Larrivee at the Maine State Prison and given to Joyce A Leonard 1999

Out of the Darkness... "Freedom Within"

Joyce A. Leonard

Dennis S. Lennon uses his artistic flair to create stationary, cards etc. to support himself while incarcerated.

These are only a few of the many exquisite drawings of Dennis Lennon – Louisiana State Penitentiary.

Stephen Mickey, a victim of Post-Polio syndrome adds his inspirational verses to the cards created by Dennis Lennon and prays that these verses of inspiration will be helpful for all who read them, ©Poetic Expressions * P.O. Box 172 * St. Naziane, WI 54232

"Thank you"

"Thank you for being
a source of strength,
A source of courage,
A beacon of light,
a tunnel of love
In reaching out to me
You dispayed concern
You showed me Love,
bringing HOPE and
a ray of sunshine."

By Stephen Mickey

"Failure"

"Now that I accept my weaknesses and accept personal responsibility for my actions, (at one time in my life I wasn't willing to correct my problem), which my failure was drugs. I let drugs discourage me. I wasn't functioning properly so therefore I wasn't thinking straight. I would punish myself with self-inflicted guilt, instead of moving on from failure to success. I had no mercy on myself. I couldn't attain my limitations and I had no respectability, so my depression deepened. I have reached the point in life that my fear of failure has led to determination to succeed and face reality. I now have the power and a sound mind as to where I should shake off the past and conquer my future by confessing. I may have to take two steps forward and one step back before making progress, but I am determined to turn my failure into victory. I render them helpless, powerless, inoperative, and ineffective to come against every stronghold and cast out the work of darkness from the enemy in my life. God has taken the things that were bad from my life (which the devil likes) and turned them around. God has taken over. He is in charge. My failure was not the end; it was just a trouble spot along the way."

By Janice Brown Lewis – Inmate at Richmond County Detention Center – Augusta, Georgia (1999)

Joyce A. Leonard

"A Letter from Zambia, Central Africa"

"I am a prisoner at the addressed prison: Leonard Sisulu, Maximum Security Prison, P.O. Box 80195 Zambia, Central Africa KABWE and I have finished 12 years here. I was baptized while in prison in 1992 with 25 other inmates. I found a ministry called the 'Remnant Evangelism Ministry' "with the primary object of spreading the Three Angels Messages to prisoners.

My life was empty, and it would always been this way if God had not placed good people in my pathway. People I would not have believed had existed before. Today I thank God that He permitted me to be in prison. Maybe it was His purpose to do His will. (Romans 8:28) Here I have been able to start a new life for myself and choose between good and evil.

First Livingston State Prison, before my conversion and my conviction, I wandered around there feeling disconnected and disoriented. At that time in my life all the loose ends of my life had come unraveled. Like Humpy Dumpty all my existence seemed like a smashed egg shell that 'all the kings' horses and all the kings' men could not put back together again.'

Every time I looked toward the windows looking out of the prison at society, life mocked me with the happy, loving world, 'reach out and touch someone' kept running around and around in my mind. Reach out and touch on someone was more like it I thought sourly. Desperation finally drove me to church in prison. I felt comfortable when I joined the Christians. I thought they would brush me off. I prepared myself for rejection, but I wasn't prepared for what I got, which was warmth, sympathy, and interest. The welcome they gave me was exhilarating. It made me feel more guilty for I was in truth not surrendered to God at all. I wasn't allowing God to lead in any way. Every day I would tell God what and how I would do, where to go and where not I would believe. I was deceiving myself, but as evangelists and pastors visited me in prison with God's Word, my heart became open to God's Word. What a radical change only God can bestow!

Today, my only desire is to serve God in every moment of my life and that the rite of baptism be a public demonstration and a symbol of rebirth to new life of obedience to sacred commandments of God, which I am doing here with the help of the Savior.

They have sentenced me to death for murder and I say that that despite spending the best of my years of my life in prison, it is nothing to be compared to the marvelous happiness of having known God. This and much more. I am willing to suffer, if necessary, to experience salvation.

What is a death sentence to me if I live with God studying and serving Him? In Romans 8:1, Paul says, 'Therefore now no condemnation to them which are in Christ Jesus, who walk not after the flesh, but after the Spirit.' In God I trust, one day…freedom. No fear overwhelms me. My only fear is offending the One Who gives us great opportunity of repenting with all one's heart, the One who forgives sin. But this is not a fear of being afraid of consequences, it stems from feeling a devotion of reverence. I obey God because today I know His power. I put myself in His hands that if it should be His will His name shall be glorified in my life for, I love Him fervently. I know that in this bosom I shall find peace and joy as I have never known until now.

I was born on 42nd Hill Drive, Naledi Harrismith, South Africa to Mr. Mlangeni Sisulu who was shot dead when war broke out in our village. My mother, a Zambian brought me here to Central Africa after my father's death. Mother married Mr. James Hamitelo who adopted me."

(This letter was written in part. It was sent to Sandra Doran who write for the "Signs of the Times" magazine. Her article "Heart of the Matter" of August 1998 inspired this letter and was shared with the readers of the "Freedom Within" newsletter.)

"The Master Craftsman"

"Often when we are so busy with our lives, we either do not see the forest through the trees or like the person who sees his reflection and forgot what he saw. (James 1:22-23) I was a Christian before I can remember, because of the way I was raised in part, and as some today would call it to be a Christian. In the reflection of my life, it becomes certain that someone or something was guiding my life.

Almost twenty years ago, my young niece and nephew, their father, his wife, and baby daughter perished in a fire on of all nights, Christmas! Naturally, my family was devastated. My sister and their mother, still have not softened their heart. It was another five years before I was able to, and then not by anything I did, as the pain and lack of understanding kept me in hatred of this unknown God. (Isaiah 55:8-11; Acts 17:23)

Several years later my wife required an emergency cesarean section, two months premature. I was fortunate enough to hold her hand as she gave birth. The miracle of birth especially in such a way really humbled me and confused me more. There had to be a God, but how could He allow such pain to enter our lives?

At once I became alarmed when I watched the doctor give my son CPR! They placed him in an incubator and rushed him by ambulance to an intensive care hospital where the doctors and nurses battled around the clock to save his life. My wife, unaware of the emergency, already had his name chosen, but I insisted that he be named, 'Joshua.' It was only later that I realized the significance of that name. – 'Jesus saves.' In time I learned they had done all that was medically possible, but my son was closer to death.

The whole week I spent arguing with this unknown God and still my son's life was hanging in the balance. In utter despair and a broken heart, {Matthew 5: 3-4) I threw myself on my face and cried out to Jesus. I did not understand many things, and I was uncertain, but it was then I gave my life to the Lord. I pleaded for my son's life in place of mine. When I visited him the next time, his condition had not changed. No matter what God does for us, no matter what we know (Romans 1:21) we refuse to live just as my son seemed to be doing. Although we have a name that lives (Revelation 3:1-3), and we must have the will to live in Christ Jesus or we too face death. As I watched my son appear to be lifeless, I had the urge to place my finger in his hand. Before when I had done this there was never a reaction, but this time he quickly clasped his little hand around my huge finger!

I was beside myself with tears of joy! Just as the Lord remembered Noah, (Genesis 8:1), He remembered me and my son. All the blind hate I had previously displayed toward Him and yet He never turned away from me. I was able to have my son removed from the life support system and hold him in my arms. But again, there was no response. I cried unto the Lord for his life once more. It was right after that he was able to begin eating and started doing all the things a healthy baby does. Unfortunately, not everyone experiences this kind of miracle, but I praise God that He chose to do this for me. I had never spent time n the Word of God. I believed as long as I did something good each day, the rest of the time I could live as I pleased.

It was just a few years later I went through a bitter divorce, and a child custody battle. I had a girlfriend and an illegitimate son, and my life was as low as it could get. When I found myself heading for prison, I was in shock that this was happening to me. I could not believe that this nightmare was actually a reality, so I took my new family and ran. We lived under assumed names, homeless, jobless, and hungry, I was led to northern Maine. My life was plentiful with lunch and dinner invitations almost daily. It was evident to me that life wasn't luck, but Divine intervention. The burdens of guilt became too much for me to bear. God was using these saints to show me agape love.

When I was arrested, I felt relieved to be released from this burden of guilt for deceiving these special people. Even the arresting officer had played a part in my life by taking me and my family to church. My boss had offered to post my high bail bond with his own money and property! I couldn't accept their gracious love. I felt I had to earn their love. They will always be special in my heart. By their love and obedience, they showed Jesus to me. They also showed me that God is truly Sovereign and He not only shapes history, but as a master craftsman (Jeremiah 18:1-11), He shapes our very lives and character.

In I Corinthians 13:13, it is written '…the greatest gift of these is *love*.' The reason it is truly the greatest is because *'God is love.'* (I John 4:8) Only His love could have led me to Caribou, ME. Only His love could come through His faithful people. It was this love that gave me the understanding of His unconditional love for me and for you. Just as the children of Israel were stubborn and God continually strived for them, I am reminded of my experiences and I will always remember that even when I fail Him, He will always love me, (Micah 7:7-8), and you are too! No matter what your circumstances my be, remember His love for you (John 3:16) is love from the '***master craftsman***.'"

(By Pryor Hall – New River Correctional Center- Reiford, Florida –
Taken from Volume 2 Issue 4 of Freedom Within 1999)

"Prisoners are Forgotten"

Prisoners are forgotten –
Oh, what a tragedy!
Time will heal all wounds.
As prisoners sit behind the cold, thick, drear prison walls.
As they dread year after year,
They are filled with hatred and fear,
With loneliness and despair.
Doesn't society even care?
Always remember the little Babe,
That died upon that hill,
And remember that Jesus said…
'You are always special in My eyes;'
As I say for one last time
a song or poem-
Prisoners are forgotten,
Oh, what a tragedy.

By Joseph J. French
MCI (Maine Correctional Institution)

Out of the Darkness... "Freedom Within"

"Thoughts from David Jack"

1999

By David Jack @ Maine State Prison

"As I come awake, I keep my eyes shut. I don't dare to open them for fear of what I will see, oh but can I live this life when I can't stand to live with me?

When I look in the mirror and see all that I can see is a misfit who is full of hate and rage, a misfortune from the start as I sit in my prison – locked away in a cage, I see what a miserable person I have become."

I do indecent acts to fill my soul of what I lost long ago."

"I never dehumanize anyone. I define life as I know it; forever denying my happiness in life, delusions, or demented, I am deserving what I get. I play the devil's advocate. I am a desperado who desires what he cannot have.

A void has taken what is left of my soul, yet I am no different from you or them. A disciple of my own personal prison is where I live.

David Jack MCI (Super Max) Warren, ME

Joyce A. Leonard

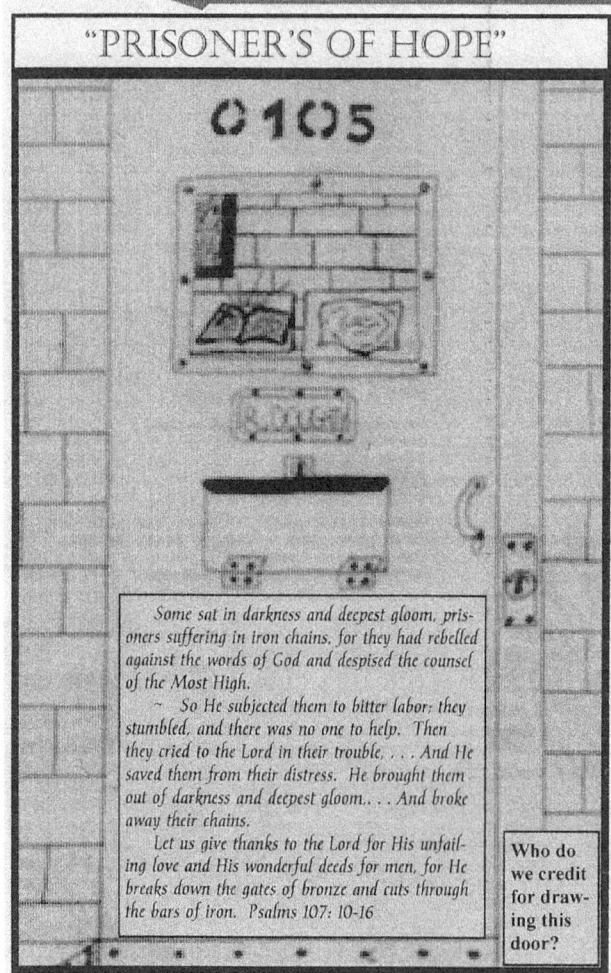

Submitted anonymously to "Freedom Within" by an inmate at Maine State Prison.

"Keep Your Faith"

"As I walk down life's long and winding roads,
I pray to God for His forgiveness before I grow old!
Jesus walked the earth to show us the way.
And through Him we talk to God, and as we kneel and pray.
So don't worry about what the devil will throw at you and me;
Just keep your faith in Jesus and He will grant you life eternally.
So on those nights when you feel nothing can be done,
Sing a praise in your head and thank God for His precious Son!
So stand straight and walk holy in God's precious sight,
And in your heart thank Jesus for being the way, truth and light."

(By Timothy Sanders – New River Correctional Center - Raiford, Florida)

"Testimony from Raybrook Federal Prison"

"My name is Franck C. and this is my testimony of how Jesus became my Lord and Savior. In August of 1990, I was arrested on some very serious charges and if convicted I would be spending many years in jail. At the time of my arrest I was 37 years old.

The first few days in jail many thoughts were going through my mnd. Only a few days before my arrest, I thought my life was going pretty well. My business was going well and I had a nice girlfriend whom I loved very much. Thoughts of my family were also going through my mind. My arrest was a very big event and it made all the newspapers and televison programs, so I knew my family was not feeling too good about that, not to mention the situation I was in.

A few days later I had a visitor, a friend I will call 'Mack' came to visit. Prior to my arrest Mack had tried a few times to share with me about being born again, but I would always cut him short by saying, 'save that for someone else.' As far as I was concerned, believing in God and going to church almost every week, and donating money, I was going to heaven, so why did I need to hear about being saved? Well, when Mack had asked me if I would mind if he shared what it means to be born again, this time I was all ears. If for any other reason, I was just happy to have some company. Little did I know that what Mack was going to share with me would change my life. He shared John 3:3 that caught my attention. When Jesus said, 'Truly, truly, I say to you, unless one is born again, he cannot see the kingdom of God.' Then he shared John 3:16 'For God so loved the world that He gave His only begotten Son, that whoever believes in Him should not persih but have everlasting life.' Mack shared a few other Scriptures as well. It all sounded good, but in all honesty I was finding it hard to believe that Jesus would come into this life and change it. Mack appreciated my being honest. He said the only way I could receive this gift is to believe salvation is free.

Later that night I was sitting in my cell and I started to think about my situation. This time my mind was out of control with thoughts of losing everything I had, and spending many years in jail. That is when I hit rock bottom. I started to think about what Mack had shared with me earlier that day and how Jesus could change my life. Before I knew it, I was on my knees pouring out my heart to God. As I did that I could feel the heaviness in my life start to be lifted. When I got up off my knees I was no longer carying a heavy load that I had just minutes ago. That is when I knew something good had taken place in my life. I have been saved a little over eight years now, although I have spent those years in jail, I must say they have been the most consistent years of my life. What started out to be the very worst day of my life turned out to be the very best day of my life and I owe it all to my Lord and Savior, Jesus Christ."

(Testimony written 3/28/99 by Franck C. sent in to "Freedom Within" from Raybrook, NY Federal Prison)

"Coerced Confession"

Told by Bobby Moore Jr Inmate at Boldoc Facility – Warren Maine 1999

June 10, 1994 was the beginning of Bobby Moore's nightmare. He lived at Ocean Point not far from Wiscasset when two sherrif's arrived late at his home that evening. He was home alone. It seems there was a big stone building on Fisherman's Island about one mile south of Ocean Point that had been broken into and a hole was burned through the floor there. Bobby was being targeted for arson.

Bobby said they hollered and sceamed at him so much that he became afraid of what they might do to him. He felt he had no choice but to sign a confession and maybe they would leave him alone. Bobby had a mental disability along with not fully comprehending the logistics of a situation so he was not capable of defending himself against the officers that interrogated him.

Bobby found himself in Lincoln Conty Superior Court paying a large sum of money for an attorney that didn't go out of his way to defend him. He lost his jury trial and felt taken advantage of from a lawyer he trusted to help him. It was June 14, 1995 when taken to MCC (Maine Correction Center) in South Windham. His stay there was five months before being taken to Maine State Prison (MSP). It was just one step following another from Lincoln County Jail for Bobby's fate.

Bobby was born October 26, 1950 in Augusta, ME. He lived with his parents and one sister, Lisa until he moved into a mobile home in 1982 on Ocean Point. He loved his little humble home and has felt abandoned and deserted since that awful day on June 14, 1994.

Bobby claims his Miranda Rights were not read to him and neither was he permitted to have an attorney present or a guardian during his interrogation. Bobby feels his freedom of choice was violated as well as his right to a fair discovery of facts. In spite of all this, Bobby maintains his belief in God and still serves Jesus. He has been transferred from Maine State Prison to Boldoc Correctional Facility which is low security. Bobby looks forward to the day when he can walk a free man and feels it has been his faith that has kept him to endure his hardships. Bobby's release date was November 7, 2000.

"The Magician"

"At chapel tonight an inmate the size of a mountain, stood to sing a song. He was Kojak, bald with an Abe Lincoln beard. His arms were covered with Swastikas, skulls and various racist remarks stood out in greenish-black ink. The tattoes marked him as Aryan Nation. One of

Joyce A. Leonard

the hundred men in chapel this night, ninety five were black. Could any maan's arms been more offensive to African Americans?

I tensed wondering what this man could possibly have to say to this particular gathering. As he turned to speak, surprise replaced tension. His face, phlegmatic and tranquil, did not fit the skin head or the racist tatoos. Across the knuckles of his left hand were the letters H-A-T-E, but his voice was only love. He spoke about a man, -The Man- who had turnd his veminous hatred to genuine love. His obvious sincerity was compelling and his laugh was contagious.

Picking up a guitar, he sang in a deep rich Burl Ives tone. Somehow this man had been changed. The man he sang about was a magician, changing a white supremist into something sweet, humble and pacific. It was not a drug (although Marx might argue that), nor was it anything artificial. – this inmates's presence would not allow for that. It was religion.

All religions begin with perception that somethig is wrong. The Jews call it lawlessness. The Christians call it sin. In Islam it is called evil. Even in Eastern religions it is so. Hindu's confess and karma (umm, excuse me, but your karma ran over my dogma!) and Buddhists acknowledge that need to be enlightened. Religion, it seems, provides a path from wrongness to war purity and lightness of heart and soul.

The religion of The Man- Jesus had extracted the vile from this man. He sang with a cleansed heart and an abundant spirit. The tattoos were all that was left of his wrongness, a harsh and permanent reminder of where he began. The Magician had transformed him. He was no longer a sinner, at least not in essence, and he was not quite a saint, but he was a kind of saint. He had not been martyred like Jude or Peter, yet something had died. It must have been the wrongness. Sometimes seekers become belivers and sometimes believers become followers and sometimes zealots. In that immaculate moment, in a room full of sinners and saints, I became something. Somewhere between the wrongness and The Magician, on a hazy road, I felt a little less heavy. It was a good feeling."

(Written by: Jeffrey Brent Hannah #K50609 Menard Correctional Center P.O. Box 711 – Menard, IL 62259)

"Holiday Spirit"

"What dors a person feel being locked down during holiday season? This is one of the toughest questions I have ever faced. How can a person completely describe an emotion and get their point across? From a personal view this is my own explanation. Thanksgiving without a doubt has to be the hardest for me. That was the time my family set all differences aside and all gathered at my grandparents for a grand feast. It was like a piece of peace and tranquility at its best. Now however all the emotional portion of that holiday is gone. The only remains of that tranquility is memories, which is a double edge sword as a person sits aand dwells on how it was and how it is. A void that is created and then filled with a nothingness, an emptiness. It cannot be described as a pain as it is beyond this. It is like being incomplete knowing there is not one thing that you can do about it. A total 'lost' feeling.

Christmas is not as bad for me. Throughout the year I will make special gifts for my family and give them at Christmas. My family will send me things that I need and want the most – a card, maybe some new jeans, and a time to call and have a long conversation with no concern of the cost, is a subject that is asked for as a present. I think the reason that Christmas is not as bad for me is because I choose it to be that way. I do not get caught up in self-pity, the depression of where I am. I do not care one bit about the materialistic part of Christmas.

Christmas is the celebration of the birth of a man who walked the earth who died for everyone's sins so they can be forgiven and saved. If that is not unconditional and limitless love, then I don't know what is! Instead of dwelling on what I am without, I choose to dwell on, I wonder what it would be like to walk with Christ our Lord, just one day while He was physically here on earth. I then spend the day observing people and their actions and reactions and interactions…wondering. Just recently I have been invited to be part of some very special people's lives and these people are special to me. We often speak of what we would like to be in priosn. Generally the negative portion of prison comes out. I am here to openly and honestly testify that some of the most compassionate, caring people are behind bars. If you ever doubt this, spend one Christmas in prison and have someone see you in pain, soon an army of people will be there to help you through this pain, as they one at a time had been there themselves.

I suppose this may not of been what was in my mind when I was asked to write one's feelings during the holidays, but how does a person describe 'feelings?' I do, however, hope and pray that not any others need to know or have the personal experience of 'holiday' behind bars. Emptiness is not an emotion anyone should experience on a holiday."

(Written and submitted by Jerry Larrivee Maine State Prison 1998)

Sharing My Lessons, I have Learned

"Do not believe the sin lie 'it won't hurt anyone.' Sin put Christ on the Cross. Sin put me in prison. Sin hurt many who trusted me.

True repentance means change. It has nothing to do with the endless cycle of sin and confession. It means changing your mind and changing your ways,

Only God can truly meet your needs, No human no matter how special he is can give us what God gives us.

Never let anything – not a paycheck or your own security stand in the way of honest accountability.

The only time you can experience God's love and peace is in obedience and brokenness.

Please don't think 'this will never happen to me.' I, at one time thought that way.

I was wrong.

(By Jeff Hannah – Shawnee Correctional Center Vienna, Ill – Taken from "Focus on the Family" Magazine Oct. 1998)

"Alethia's Hope and Prayer"

"God is our Savior, Master and Lord.
He truly wants us on one accord.
God is coming and we don't know when,
Be ready My people for we are nearing the end.
Though Christ Jesus is our only way out,
We must trust Him without a doubt.
He is all the answers and He knows what is best,
Had we lived rightly by God,
Our life wouldn't be such a mess.
Our father is testing us to see if we are strong.
He knows what is right and is never wrong.
I thank you Father for bringing me to jail.
For sparing my life and sparing me from hell.
You had to stop me because I was moving to fast.
I am now a new creation at last,
And I am through with the past.
I aim to serve you, most definitely please;
Forgive me Lord, for not bending my knees.
Help me Lord to do what is right.
I am no longer in the dark but walking in the light."

(Written and submitted by Alethia M. Vann – Richmond County Detention Center – Augusta, Georgia 1999)

Following quotes sent in annonymously by Inmate at Maine State Prison – Supermax

- "I have learned silence from the talkative, Tolerance from the intolerant and kindness from the unkind; yet strange, I am ungrateful to those teachers!"
- "A man of words and not of deeds is like a garden full of weeds."
- "We all have strength to endure the misfortunes of others."

Joyce A. Leonard

"Keep Your Head Up"

"Lately I find myslef in a daze, making excuses to stay in bed,
Even though I could be doing stuff.
I guess you could say I ain't tryin' hard enough…sometimes I feel so ashamed, and I ask myself, 'Who is to
blame?' I have come to the point
where enough is enough! From this day forward,
I will keep my head up."

(Written and submitted by Wilfred Clark – Louisiana State Penitenuary – Angola, LA 2001)

"Only the Strong Will Survive"

"In the Bible, Jesus our Savior told the story about a wise builder and a naïve one. The wise one fastidiously dug deep, so he could build a firm foundation on the soil. The not so wise one wanted to build his castle quickly. So he built on top of the ground and didn't worry about anything else but finishing first.

Common sense should tell you that if you build any type of building without worrying about it's foundation, nine times out of ten, you will finish soon. The fact that you are going to look pretty sharp to a passerby who may see you on your patio, maxin' and relaxin.'

Folks will say, 'Look how fast, he finished that crib. He must really know his stuff! The other dude must be crazy over there hammering away with so much sweat and effort for a place that looks identical to his.' Then a storm comes along. Massive floods wash away the fast paced house that went up so soon. It wasn't built on solid ground. On the other hand, the other house stands tall and rides the storm out like a champ! Who do you think is the crazy one?

Sometimes isn't our faith like that? It's continually tempting to build faith quickly and easily. Who wants to dig, get dirty or work hard in the blazing sun? It is rare you find people going around saying; 'I just love your foundation!' Actually foundations go unnoticed. Our human nature wants to avoid foundations completely and go directly to what folks like to see; the high profile stuff, the glamour and the spectacular for example, if a minister asks a couple of members to lead worship service, all kinds of hands would pop up in the air. But as soon as he asks if someone can volunteer to help clean simple church restrooms or tending to another's children in the nursery, then all of a sudden everyone seems to be busy.

Somehow we seem to have more than enough time to lead a group of people, but not enough to help with practical stuff, like restrooms. Why? Do I need to say? We look at these things as - 'Where is the fame?' 'Where's the glory in this?' 'Where is the reward in cleaning toilets for Jesus?'

Simple, Jesus said very clearly; 'Without laying solid ground structure, we will be swept away by some tide of life.' You don't want that to happen to you... I thought not! We dare not start anything in the name of the Lord without first digging deeply before we build up. He doesn't want us left in ruins and misery when the great storm comes. He wants us to be safe inside His stabalized well-built castle with Him."

(Written and submitted by Eric D. Calvin of Louisiana State Penitentuary Angola, LA 2001)

(Drawing created by Eric D. Calvin Louisiana State Penitentiary, Angola, LA)

Eric Calvin is now on parole after a 170 year sentence, he is a free man after 25 years incarcerated. He has turned his life to become a real man of God and has made incredible efforts to be trusted, show responsibility, and to become a good citizen. Praise the Lord who transforms, redeems and gives "second chances."

"A Second Chance"

"People…what I write is not a poem, nor a story, or even a quote from the Bible. No. What it is, is only something that I happened to forget along the way. Friends and family are the essence of life, and the purpose of existence is caring and commitment. In the past, I've let dowm many of whom I care for, and for this I am very sorry. This also is where I also ask for that second chance. and I pray that it will be God's will to give it."

(Written by By Inmate William Peters MSP – Thomaston, ME 2001)

"Testimony of Robert Clark"

"I grew up luckily with a good mother and father. My father died of a drinking disorder when I was about two years old. Then somewhere down the line my mom met a good man, who became like a real father to me. My mom always tried to get close to me, but one of us sooner or later would push the other away. So as the years went by, it was hard to love one another, even though the love was there, for we were both too scared to show it.

It seems, in school, I was always trying to impress everyone, especially the girls. I started running around with a gang because I saw the brotherhood they had for one another being always quick to defend the other person and to help others do anything even if it meant to take a tiff from another man just because of the colors he had on. I was a runaway, running the streets in and out of detention centers and programs. I was getting worse and worse and gettng involved in shootings, robberies, fighting, gettting shot at and having sex with different women. It was fun to me, and I didn't care.

I thought life was a game. Even when I had been beat up and didn't have anywhere to go, I went back to my mom's house for comfort, but I was still stuck in the world I wanted to be in.

I had a good woman trying to stand by me, but I would not let my heart go out to anyone, not even when she was pregnant with my son. I still would not listen. I was confused, but I felt I had my own life and I was going to live it the way I wanted to, and no one was going to stop me, but I was wrong.

Finally, thinking I was on top of the world with girls, cars, apartment, and money; I thought I had it all, but there was an empty spot in my heart. I tried many different drugs – weed and cocaine were the ones I felt gave me what I needed. One night I robbed a store at gun point, and I robbed the same store four or five days later. I didn't care anymore. I felt I was the 'the man,' but I was still trying to be somebody I wasn't.

Two weeks after the robberies, I was arrested for armed robbery with a firearm. During my stay at the County jail, my son ws born. I was proud of my girlfriend. My eyes were opened when he was born, and this was my chance to love someone without a front. My eyes were opened to the Lord at this time also. Men had been planting seeds and I was saved.

When the judge sentenced me to 120 months in prison, I lost my faith. My plans were put on hold and I couldn't do anything. Somehow I had let a man take control of my life and I could't understand it. I was a gangster, dope dealer, robber, but here I was in the county jail and couldn't leave it if I wanted and I had to obey the rules. I was so mad because I was going to try to do right for me, my girl, and my son, but I wasn't putting God first and He knew I wasn't ready. I was sent to Baker Correctional Institution where I was involved in another gang activity. Violence between our gang and another occurred, and I was sent to New River East. I thank God for having me sent here in 1999. I rededicated my life to Christ. The Lord used three good vessels, Gregory, Samuel, and Mamie, who helped me to crawl until I could walk. Without them I wouldn't be writing this testimony right now. May God bless them.

They took the time to show me that God loves me and I was blind, but now I see. God reached down to my my soul and filled that spot in my heart with my love for Jesus and He restored the relationship between me and my mom. She is not only my mother, but now she is my friend too.

I also know that when noone else is there, God was and He's the One who restored that relationsship for He can do all things. I also realize I have no need for color, signs or gang knowledge.

I once heard a song, 'Is there a heaven for a gangster?' I told myself, 'Ya, if your leader is God.' We don't need a man to be our leader, for he could lead us wrong. We need the Almighty Father, God, for He is truth who sees no color and has all knowledge. The truth will set you free for it saved a man like me who once was lost, but now enduring to the end."

> "For we shall overcome by the blood of the Lamb, and the words of our testimony..." Amen (Revelation 12:11)

(Robert Clark was an inmate at Raiford, Florida Correctional Institution.)

"Choose How to Start Your Day Tomorrow"

Michael is the kind of guy you love to hate. He Is always in a good mood and always has something to say! If someone would ask him how he is doing, he would reply, 'If I were better, I would be twins.' He was a natural motivator. If an employee was having a bad day, Michael was there to tell him or her how to look on the positive side of the situation. Seeing his style really made me curious, so I went up to Michael, and asked him, 'You can't be a positive person all the time so how do you do it?' Michael replied, "Each morning I say to myself, 'you have two choices today. You can choose to be in a good mood or you can chose to be in a bad mood. I choose to be in a good mood. Every time something bad happens, I can choose to be a victim or I can choose to learn from it. Every time someone comes to me complaining, I can choose to accept their complaining or I can point out the positve side of life. I choose the positive side of life.'

"Yeh right, It's not that easy,' I protested. 'Yes, it is,' Michael insisted. 'Life is about choices. When you cut away the junk, every situation is a choice. You choose how to react to situations. You choose how people affect your mood. Your bottom line is your choice how you live your life.' I reflected on what Michael said. Soon thereafter, I left the lower industry to start my own business. We lost touch, but I often thought about him when I made a choice about life instead of reacting on it.

Several years later, I heard Michael was involved in a serious accident, falling 60 feet from a communication tower. After 18 hours of surgery and weeks in intensive care, Michael was released from the hospital with rods placed in his back. I saw Michael about six months after the accident. When I asked him how he was, he replied, "If I was better I would be twins. Wanna see my scars?' I declined to see his wounds, but I did ask what went through his mind when the accident took place.

'The first thing was the well-being of my soon to be born daughter,' Michael replied. 'Then as I lay on the ground, I remembered I had two choices. I could choose to live, or I could choose to die. I chose to live.'

'Weren't you scared? Did you lose consciousness?' I asked. Michael continued...'the paramedics were great. They kept telling me I was going to live. But when they wheeled me into the ER and I saw the expressions on the faces of the doctors and the nurses, I got really scared. In their eyes, I read, 'he's a dead man.' I knew I had to take action.' 'What did you do?' I asked. 'Well, there was a big burly nurse shouting questions at me, ' said Michael. She asked if I was allergic to anything. 'Yes,' I replied. The doctors and nurses stopped working as they waited for my reply. I took a deep breath and yelled, 'Gravity.' Over their laughter, I told them, I am choosing to live. Operate on me as if I am alive and not dead.' Michael lived, thanks to the skill of his doctors, but also because of the amazing attitude. I learned from him that every day is a choice to live fully. Attitude afer all, is everything. 'Therefore don't worry about tomorrow for tomorrow will worry about itself.' Each day has enough trouble of its own.' (Matthew 6:34) After all today is tomorrow that you worried about yesterday."

(Submitted by Frank Morgan – Inmate at Arizona State Prison 2002)

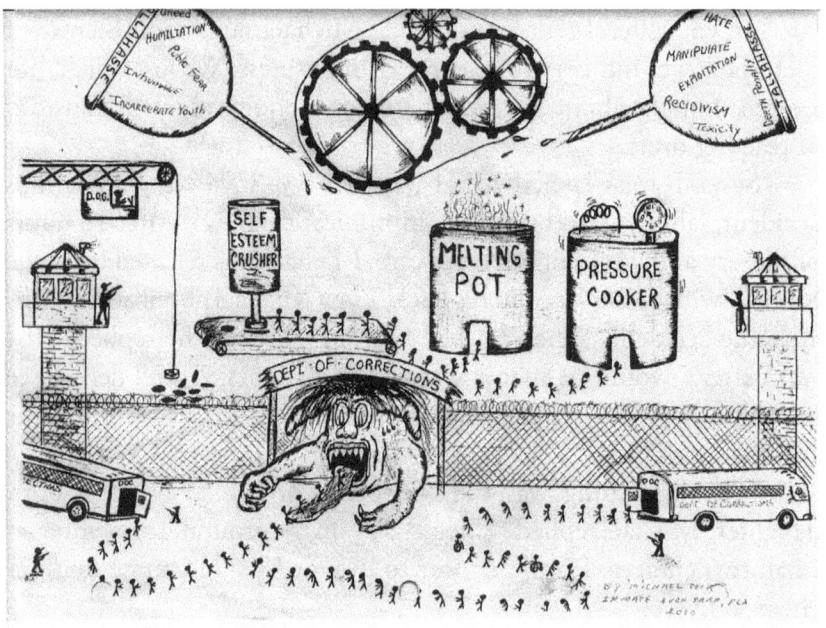

(Drawing created by Michael Cook -Inmate at Avon Park, Florida 2000)

Quote

"If we work upon marble it will perish, if on brass, time will erase it. If we rear temples, they will crumble into dust; but if we work upon human minds and imbue them with the just fear of God, and love for our fellowmen, we engrave on these tables something that will brighten to all eternity." ~Daniel Webster~

Rage

CHAPTER FIVE

> Written by Michael Braiser Inmate @ Maine State Prison while in Thomaston, ME 2001. This is a 5-part series complied for "Freedom Within." This presents an honest look at anger and how rage develops if it is not controlled.

"Why do others get angry while others like myself RAGE? What is the difference between anger and rage? These are just some of the questions I am going to address. The answers to some questions are based on my own past experiences with rage. It is important to remember that though some of the characteristics of rage and anger are the same, we as individuals are all different and deal with the same issue of rage differently. It is not my intention to find you answers or tell you the answers for your problem. I won't.

The answer lies somewhere within you. It is my intention to share with you, my battles with rage and how I learned to cope with it. I hope and pray that somewhere amongst these words that you will be able to relate to my story. I offer only suggestions as to how to deal with rage as I learned what works for me in my experience. Just like everything in life there is more than one kind of rage, I would like to focus on the two I am most familiar with.

1. **The Outward Rage** - The rager that lashes out verbally and physically.
2. **The Inward Rage** – The rager who is quiet and allows the rage to boil and fester inside himself, but most often ends up hurting himself.

Is there s difference between anger and rage? I would say, most certtainly. Let's take a look at what the Webster Dictionary has to say.

ANGER: A strong feeling of displeasure, resentment or hostility. This is a noun. To make or become angry. Anger now becomes an action verb instead of just a feeling or emotion.

RAGE: 1. Violent, explosive anger 2. Furious intensity. 3. A fad or craze. (This is a noun) Raged or raging – to speak or act in violent force. This becomes a verb.

We can see by these definitions that anger and rage are one in the same.. So why do I say that anger and rage are different? It is the level of intensity that sets anger and rage apart. For *example*: We have regualr rain and windstorms.

Usually I don't pay much attention to them. However, when the intensity of that rain and wind hits in such a violent magnitude that is is no longer classified as just a storm, it becomes a hurricane or a tornado. That is the difference between anger and rage. While you prepare for a rainstorm, it is harder to prepare for a hurricane especially if it hits with no warning. Another way you can distinguish anger from rage is an emotion that comes and goes without our say so. I just happens that RAGE can be summoned on command if necessary. Let me try to explain why I say that. Rage unlike anger can be used as a self-protection mechanism. When we are in a rage everything ceases to exist. There is no fear, no emotion at all besides a white hot, burning rage. Consequenses cease to be a deterrent. Rage gives in to false courage.

There are times in my life (mostly during the four years I was abused by my step-father) that I was dependent on my rage to survive. I could work myself up into a fury. It wasn't enough just to be angry because I was still rational, though I was angry I could still feel the fear and the physical pain; whereas while I was in a rage, I felt nothing physical or emotional.

Don't misconstrue what I am saying – rage is for most people uncontorllable. Once they have allowed themselves to be overwhelmed by their anger, it then takes control over them, but some people like myself can go into a rage at will.

How or why do some people become ragers? For me it was a self-defense. A self protection mechanism.

RAGE - PART 2 -*Understanding the Addiction* - In this part of the rage series, I want to help you understand how I became addicted to rage and came to depend on it. Let's take a look at the alcoholic and compare the similarities to the process of addiction and dependence.

The first comparison I want to make is the false courage we seem to get when we are under the influence of alcohol or rage. Alcohol has a way of turning a mouse into a roaring lion. We tend to do things when we are drunk when under sober circumstances we wouldn't even think about doing, let alone do them. It is the same way with rage. It gives us a false courage that enables us to do things we wouldn't do in a calm and rational state of mind. They say alcohol lowers inhibitions. Rage obliterates them.

Like cocaine, adrenaline can get you pumped up. It gets the blood racing like the speed of light. You get the feeling like you are super strong, so strong in fact, it makes Superman look like a sissy in his blue tights and red oversized bib. Adrenaline is a hormone in the human body. The medical term is epinephrine. An adrenaline hormone that constricts blood vessels and raises blood pressure. I am not a doctor and I do not fully understand the purpose of adrenaline but I know this much, adrenaline can be classified as a natural drug, becaue when you get high from it, that high or rush is extremely addicting.

There are some people labeled thrill seekers. These people usually go to extreme measures to experience an adrenaline high. They do things like jump out of airplanes, bungee jump, or wrestle alligators. But they are not the only people that seek the adrenaline high. On a smaller level you have people who go on roller coasters or go into haunted houses or even rent a scary movie. So now you may get to see how addicting adrenaline can be.

As a rager, I became addicted to the intensity of anger and the adreneline I was feeling. Like the alcoholic, after a while of being addicted and a long time of abusing the drink, I soon became dependent on my rage. The only way I knew how to react to a bad situation was by going into a rage. Alcohol has a way of making our problems so we don't have to deal with them and rage does the same thing. Instead of facing the fear of pain I would put myself into a rage where I felt absolutely nothing. It was instant gratification.

Also, lke the alcoholic, we tend to lose control over our emotions. We do things we don't remember, things we wouldn't do sober, things that we most often regret later. Rage can control a person so completely that you would swear he was a different person. One of the scary things about a rager it is not a deterent for him. Consequences mean nothing. The only thing that matters is the immediate release of that burning anger P.I.G.(Personal Immediate Gratifiacation).

RAGE - Part 3

"In this part of RAGE, I am taking a different angle. We have already shown that rage is anger at the extreme, but what causes that anger? What leads up to becoming angry and eventually becoming a rager? I have learned from counseling that we experience at least one emotion if not several before becoming angry, but anger can come on so quick that unless you know what you are looking for, you can skip right over it. So let's take a look at the possible situation and see if we can identify the emotions that occur before becoming angry.

Let's say your friend, Spot and you were discussing politics, and Spot doesn't agree with your views. You believe that President Clinton is not smoking dope, war draft skipping, a womanizer who has been a poor leader and role model for our country, and Spot says to you, 'What? You think you are perfect? You think that your dirty socks don't stink? You self-rightous bleep, bleep, bleep!' All of a suden you become angry with your friend, Spot – let's stop right here. It is clear why you are angry – your friend all of a sudden wasn't so friendly and he began to insult you and call you names. But even before you became angry, you most likely felt hurt. Stung by the verbal tongue lashing. Maybe you felt rejected by the way Spot rejected you. There is also a possibility that Spot hit a nerve, and you are feeling insecure. Maybe Spot is right - low self-esteem.

But most often we don't recognize or acknowledge those feelings first. We think the first emotion we feel is anger. When in reality we experienced several emotions before becoming angry. All of this took place in the span of a heart beat. With a rager like myself, I am usually feeling these emotions but at an extreme level and they burst into a corruptive fit, with a fury like that of the wrath of God.

This amount of anger is not healthy. It is not healthy physically because it could cause any number of health problems ranging from high blood pressure, headache, hyperventilating, to heart attacks. Blood vessels could explode and you could injure yourself internally like causing ulcers. All of this is caused just by allowing ourselves to be worked into a rage after we lash out which can cause bruises, broken bones and not just our own."

Rage in the Spiritual Aspect - Part 4

"With a rager, like myself, I am usually feeling these emotions, but at an extrme level and they burst out in a conniption fit, and a great amount of fury. This amount of anger is not healthy. It is not healthy physically, mentally, emotionally or spiritually. To commit the smallest amount of sin is to commit them all. To become that angry and to go out of control is being disobedient to God, and we live in danger of not being reconciled with out heavenly Father. If we are lashing out at other people, or even ourselves, we definitely aren't showing forgiveness to the people who have hurt us.

Jesus summed it up when He taught in two commandments: 'Love the Lord thy God with all thy heart, mind, and strength.' (Matthew 22:37), and 'Love thy neighbor as thyself.' (Matthew 19:19) If you do not forgive those who trespass against you, how then can your Father in heaven forgive you? It will be measured back to you according to how much you give here on earth. Believe me, when I tell you, I know how hard it is to let go of rage. Although rage is a learned emotion, at times it feels like it was born in our genetic make-up. I don't believe we will ever get rid of the rage we have embraced for so long. It is just like alcoholics just because they haven't had a drink in 10 years doesn't mean they are cured of their alcoholism. Sure it gets easier with time, and practice not to want that drink so urgently, but the instant they pick up that first drink again, they will soon discover they are still alcoholics. I believe that applies to the rager. We can learn coping mechanisms, and actually learn how to let go of the anger, before it becomes rage, but if we don't practice management skills every day then we are in danger of allowing ourselves to be worked up into a rage. I have learned that if I let a seed harbor in my heart for even an hour, then I am putting myself at risk for a blow up. We need to exercise that feeling of ardor.

How do we do this? Only when we live day by day, or in a ragers case, from situation to situation practicing anger management skills, and immediately letting go of that anger. Do not stuff the feeling away. Get yourself under control and deal with the feeling right then and there. Admit out loud to yourself how you are feeling, because once you recognize the true feeling and accept it, then it better enables you to get your emotions in perspective and you are better able to deal with them."

Rage Part 5 How to Stop Raging

Jesus tells us clearly not to let the sun go down while we are still angry or have a grudge against somebody. Jesus knows the danger of allowing the sin of anger to fester in our hearts. In fact, Jesus spoke severely about having anger toward others. It is the same as murder in God's eyes. And all anger leads to death (spiritual death) if we don't repent, let go of the anger and ask forgivenesss. So you see how unhealthy rage can be, both physically and spiritually? So how do we change from being a rager? How do we stop raging when it has become like a second skin to our lives? How do we let go of the emotional control over us?

I won't pretend I have all the answers for you. In fact, I struggle with rage. I have gone from being a very outward, violent rager, though I have learned some coping skills to help me deal with my struggle with rage. Any time we really want something we work really hard to gain it, and that is the simple fact about anything in life, and it is the same with ragers. We have to really want to change to give up that rage and all the things that it represents like the false security, false courage, an addicting high or an adreneline rush. Do you sincerely want to let go of your rage? Are you truly seeking a happier, healthier, better life all the way around? If so then prepare to do the same hard work. I have a few suggestions on how to start down to the road to recovery.

You have probably already taken the first step by now which is admitting you do have a problem with rage. Acceptance of the weakness is half of the battle because it takes a strong person to admit that he or she has faults. The second step goes with the first, which is honesty. You must be brutally honest with yourself and that goes with loving and respecting yourself. If you lie to yourself long enough, you actually lose sight of the truth and you won't he aable to tell the truth from the lies. But you cannot lie to God. So it is absolutely vital that no matter what it is or how it makes you feel that you be completletly honest with yourself, for you have everything to gain.

The third step was and still is one of the hardest steps for me, which is to stop feeling sorry for yourself and stop making excuses. If any of you are like me, you probably have the 'I'm entitled to ' attitude. I am entitled to be angry at him because he insulted me or I am entitled to strike out at her because she hit me first. I am entitled to hold a grudge against him because I already forgave him three times before. Well, you are entitled to feel angry, but that is it. You are entitled to do something positive with your anger, even if it's just letting go, but you are not entitled to have an attitude, to judge, condemn or even to seek justice, which is revenge. The attitude has to go and we need to learn to love through our anger and hurt. I know it is not easy, but I already told you this was going to be tough."

"We can do all things through Christ Jesus Who strengthens us and with Him all things are possible." (Phillippians 4:13, Matthew 19:26)

"From the Halls of Death Row"

CHAPTER SIX

Drawing by Allan Shane Robinson MSP 1999

"Cruelty Within the Halls of Death Row"
(Civil Action suit against TDCI-ID)
by Bobby Ray Hopkins – Death Row – Huntsville, Texas 1999

"Most, if not all of you are aware that US District Judge William Justice just recently handed down another decision in the ongoing saga of unusual conditions within Texas Prison system.

While the judge conceded that some improvements have been made, gross constitutional violations still exist, especially in adminstration segregation units which is where death row is headed. The following is what the Judge had to say about such units:"

> "*Texas administrative segregation units violate (the prisoners' constitional rights to protection against cruel and unusual punishment) through extreme deprivation, which causes profound and obvious psychological pain and suffering. Texas' administrative segregation units are virtual incubators of psychosis-seeding illness in otherwise healthy inmates and exacerbating illnesses in those already suffering from mental infirmities.*"
>
> "*According to Dr. Henry Haney, of the perhaps dozens of prisons he has visited and studied in his career, Texas' ad-seg were worse than others around the country. Dr. Haney responded: 'The bedlam which ensued each time I walked out into one of those units, the number of people who were screaming, who appeared to be disturbed, the existence of people who were smeared with feces, the intensity of the noise as people began to shout and ask, 'Please come over here. Please help me.' It was shattereing as I discussed this atmosphere with the people who worked there. I was told there was nothing at all unusual about what I was seeing.'*
>
> *Dr. Haney reported one instance in which he happened to see a man removed from his cell after having cut the veins in his arms and ankles. Again, Dr. Haney was told by prison employees that such occurrances happened regularly. According to Dr. Haney, 'the level of desperation and despair in that particular facility as I saw it on that day, I was there, was unparalled in my experience.'*

Breed visited the ad-seg units of each of the prison units he found. He found Texas ad-seg system of inmates being moved into the ad-seg system were put into Level III, the level with the most severe restrictions. Breed found 'no correctional justification whatsoever,' for a system that immediatley places a prisoner in a situation with nothing left to lose.

Emphasizing that he did not report on borderline mentally ill patients, but only on inmates who would be found mentally ill by any reasonable physiatrist, Dr. Jurczak testified that he identified 15-20 'fluidly psychotic' individuals in administative segregation. 'The patients demonstrated unequivical signs and symptoms of a serious mental disorder, predorminantly that of schizophrenia.' Dr. Jurczak found that many of these individuals were not identified as mentally ill patients to administration segregation, who had been identified as such by TDCI. Some were receiving care and some were not.

Dr. Jurczak led the court through descriptions of his encounters with a number of the inmates in ad-seg that he identified as mentally ill. A number of the prisoners had free world records of mental illness. The behavoirs he reported included paranoid thoughts, looseness of association, and pressured speech. One inmate scrubbed to remove imaginary bugs from his skin. Others incessantly talked to themselves. While others were "frequent flyers" who frequently attempted suiside, and had been frequently placed into suicide watch. Another was a young man referred to him by other inmates. The inmate had been smearing his feces for several years. When Dr. Jurczak tried to interview him, the inmate was incoherently giggling, mumbling, and looking around. According to his records, this inmate was not identified as mentally ill, and was not being treated. Dr. Jurczak recognized the possibility that such behaviors were secondary gain, but stated, 'I think with thirty years of practicing psychiatry in many, many prisons, if these guys pull the wool over my eyes then they are pretty damn good.'

Dr. Jurczak also explained that, in his expert opinion, Texas' administrative segreation system harmed mentally ill inmates. 'Such inmates,' he said 'need contact and social stimuli.' More generally, Dr Jurczak testified that the ad-seg system is destructive to all its occupants. 'I think it is a very destructive system. And I have been in many, many systems…and I have never seen one as repressive as I have seen in TDCJ.'

We need not look any further than Monty Delk, Emanuel Kemp, Charles Mines, Syed Rabbani and Raymond Riles to realize that men here amongst us also have mentally crumbled beneath the weight of our appalling life conditions of isolation segregation, neglect and institutional repression. Over the years Judge Justice has constantly demonstrated alarm and digust over cruel and unusual conditions inside of Texas prisons. He made it unmistakedly clear that prisons are meant to house, not to torture, when he said '... this court has sentenced more offenders...then it cares to remember. However, an offender is sentenced to a term of imprisonment, an offender should not be sentenced to a term of enslavement by gangs, rape, abuse, by predatory inmates, or excessive force by prison employees...' But the judge cannot help us with our condition if we do not turn his attention to the state of our condition. Meaning, we must bring before him our complaints – our collective grievances. But this will never be, unless we first surmount to a major obstacle that stands in our path – between us and the court. But whatever our feelings, the reality is this:

The original 1972 Ruiz class action suit did not include death row. It origintaed in the general population and included death row as an add on in 1980. March 1, 1999 judgement handed down by William Wayne Justice is but a continuation of RUIZ, it's primary focus still on the general population.

However, Hank Skinner filed a law suit on abuse by prison guards, false disciplinary action, improper classification, etc., etc., in the exclusive interest of Texas Death Row. It was very timely as it came on the heels of Judge Justice latest opinion, which gives tremendous credibility to the issues raised which would be our suit, not Hank's.

Remember this: Victory in whatever measure is inevitably won by the people, and it is we, the prison masses, who constitute the people in this world by concrete, steel and razor wire. As organizers, who do not put personal differences before the people's needs, we support this suit in the interest of the people, and of course we ask others to join for this reason alone.

In Revolutionary Solidarity P.U.R.E. (People United Reaching Everyone)

Special Note~ Justice Wayne Justice was appointed to the Federal Bench of the Eastern District of Texas by President Lyndon B. Johnson in 1968. He was very instrumental in uncovering brutal conditions in the Texas Prison System. He died at the age of 89 – October 16, 2009

IF You Support Capital Punishment –

"In a system run by humans, and therefore prone to human error, if you support capitol punishment, you accept the fact that some of the people executed will be innocent.

As more and more teenagers are being tried as adults, if you support capitol punishment, you accept the fact that some of the people executed will be children. Because knowing right from wrong disqualifies an offender from using an insanity defense. If you support capitol punishment, you accept the fact that some of the people executed will be mentally ill or mentally retarded" (the term now is mentally challenged).

"In a society that clamors for victims' rights and compassion for the innocent, if you support capitol punishment, you accept the fact that pain and suffering will be inflicted on those who have commited no crime, the family and friends of the offender.

In an age where more and more Americans distrust 'the punishment,' you accept the fact that it is the poor who are executed and that the race of the victim does more to determine who gets the death sentence than the crime itself."

"In a country that seeks to decrease violence on television, on the streets, and in the family, if you suppport capitol punishment, you accept the fact that our children will learn that killing is the solution to society's problems.

In a world that cries out for peace and understanding, if you support capitol punishment, you have made a judgement that thousands of incarcerated Americans, (about whom you only know about what the media has told you), are no longer human, are no longer children of God, and are incapable of change, reconcilliation or redemption, and the family of the murder victims are incapable of forgiveness."

(As of 1999) "Seven years ago, my uncle was murdered. My uncle's killer is still alive, serving a life sentence, I thank God that the brutal, irrational crime that ended my uncle's life did not result in another senseless killing." (J.Z.)

Jesus was once asked for His support of the Death Penalty.
His reply was, "Let one who is without guilt cast the first stone."

(Taken from Volume 2 Issue 4 of "Freedom Within")

The American Holocaust

continued by Bobby Ray Hopkins – Death Row Livingston, Texas

"Locked up behind walls that don't move and behind doors, with steel bars marking its strength because of my weakness. This place is a new age concentration camp and it is legal. The politicians and public authorize its existence with their vows and signatures.

Kidnapped from the streets, as if an animal taken from the wild or from its natural habitat, and placed in an enviroment unfamiliar to the one I am used to seeing, and being around. I have been sent to a place where strict rules and regulations are enforced and placed on me on a daily and constant basis. No matter what the situuation, I am always considered to be wrong and the officers on the shift, and supervisors are always presumed to be right. Regardless of what the situation may be or the circumstances, that follow, I will be set up and punished for something that was created by the system and its staff.

Once sent here, I am shut in a tiny cubicle (5X9 cage), I must now call my home as I am only allowed to come out to shower, which usually takes 4-5 minutes to complete, because I am rushed in and hurried out, and if I disobey then the water will be turned off and I will be accused of disobeying an order and written a disciplinary case, which is then taken to the Inner- Departmental Unit court, and given even more punishment or stricter restrictions. Also if an order is disobeyed, I risk being run in by the guards with heavily suited armor, shields, billy clubs, mud traction boots and other riot gear.

Anytime I am allowed to come out of my cell, my hole in the wall, when I get my one-hour of recreation four days a week. For any other time has to be urgent or special trip to the infirmary or a visit that would fall under those categories.

My life is so routine and somewhat predictable because everything is done over and over again on a daily, weekly and monthly basis.

A few years ago I learned to count the steps from my cell to the shower, (which is 6 steps) then the steps from my cell to the single man recreation yard, (which is about 50) and that includes the climb up and down a flight of stairs that I have to go down while I am handcuffed and escorted by two guards each time I leave my cell.

I am a level two inmate. That is my status. I am not even referred to by my name anymore, and if someone should slip and even call me by my name, I automatically get suspicious of the person. This institution and administration consider me a number. The name 'Bobby' or 'Hopkins' rarely comes up. I am called #999101.

It's like Hitler did with the Jews in the Nazi camps in Germany, and other parts of Europe. He killed them in mass numbers and degraded them as not being from the human race, stripping them of their rights and family values. He starved them to death and buried them in large tombs or mass graves.

In the year 1997 alone, there were 48 executions in the United States as a whole. Texas was responsible for 37 of these of the 48 executions. I live on the most notorious and infamous death row of them all. As each day passes me by, it isn't getting any better, it has only gotten worse.

I am a very strong individual, but even the strongest of men can't take the cruel and unusual punishment that is being handed out in these dungeons on death row. I sometimes sit back and ask myself, 'How can it be that people can treat other people this way?' The only thing I can come up with is that there really is a Lucifer, and right now he has really come to test my faith and claim my life because I refuse to be one of his disciples. There are a handful of good guards that work here, but the number of bad ones who are programmed and conditioned to carry out the evil institutional rule, out number the good ones by a large margin.

Whether the day is quiet or active, the extra curricular activity begins each day at the crack of dawn and repeats itself the same way throughout the entire year. While most Americans are home sleeping, the turmoil in my life continues to boil and melt in a pot of total chaos and destruction, regardless of the outcome of the day, I live and cannot leave.

On a daily basis I live around incarceration, dehumanization, injustice, oppression, genocide, hatred, vengence, and misuse of public authority. I can now realize how the Jews must have felt while in those concentration camps during the hallocaust because of my own personal experience of being denied freedom, treated like an animal, and locked up waiting for my number to come up and life to end.

I must tell you personally, it is a very scary feeling to know my death is planned, as well as arranged, but in a way that is unthought of to the hman mind. They say it costs a lot more to house then to execute a condemned man, but I have also heard that the Texas executioner only really gets a set salary, and the poisoned chemicals that are pumped through peoples veins and bodies are the same chemicals that are equal to liquid Drano, rat poison, and cyanide.

My mind is strong, my body is strong, but because these chemicals are made with acids and other oxidants, they will surely devour my veins and overpower the flow of blood and burst into my heart.

The reason why the United States Court has reinstated the death penalty in 1982 because they ruled lethal injection, when applied properly, was not cruel and unusul punishment and that it is pain free. Here is my question, 'Who has been pumped full of chemicals, died and come back to tell them it was harmless and painless?' I would very much like to meet that person, and shake their hand because they knew that for a fact, then they would market that method of procedure and people who are fully afraid of painful death would be lined up to get a piece of the sure shot method.

As I end this story and tragic ordeal, I know what I am talking about is real for it has happened to so many people. I just pray that it doesn't happen to me and I pray that before it does, that a higher force from above will step down and take control amd stop these people from tinkering with my life." (Written January 18, 1999 by Bobby Ray Hopkins and submitted to Freedom Wuthin Newsletter)

Executions

"The death penalty is becoming the vie of political candor. Several times a week it is on the pages of the newspaper and quips of either leniency or the demand of death programing the need of seeking the pros and cons of such an act.

George W. Bush of Texas confirms that there 'are no innocent inmates being executed in Texas' and he 'favors capital punishment as a deterrent of crimes,' citing his reasoning as 'I believe it sends a chilling message that there is a consequence to your actions.' This was an open statement in the local Maine paper of Saturday May 27, 2000 in the Lewiston Daily Journal.

Yet, even though Mr. Bush makes his bold statement, the internet makes equally bold statements that are backed with factual evidences and poured out on computer monitors for the world to explore. The Justice Project Website states this: 'For every seven executions conducted in the last 25 years, one innocent person has been convicted and sentenced to death. Regardless of whether or not you support the death penalty, we can all agree that the execution of an innocent person, should be the 'ultimate nightmare.' (Information provided by Justice Project Website (http//:www.thejusticeproject.org).

In New Hampshire, Govenor Jeanne Shaheen proudly states that their 'statute is designed to make carrying out the death penalty extraordinarily dificult.' The Lewiston Daily Journal quotes in the May 20, 2000 issue that Governor Shaheen quoted Jimmy Carter and his wife Roslynn as saying,

'As you know, there is no evidence that the death peanalty deters heinous crimes, and it has been found that a number of those on death row, in Ohio and other states, have been found to be innocent, primarily by DNA tests.' New Hampshire has not executed anyone in 61 years (stated in 2000) and has no one on death row. The story continues in the Lewiston Journal on the same report of the incident of Richard Buchanan 'who was wrongly accused of raping and murdering the six year old daughter of his live-in girlfriend in 1997.' Atttorney General Phillip McLaughlin faced a public outcry when he decided not to charge Buchanan with capital murder. But public evidence eventually forced prosecutors to drop all charges. Buchanan who spent six months n jail became the poster boy for death penalty opponents. A former neighbor James Dale was convicted of the murder and sentenced 60 years in prison.

'This is a true example why you should not have the death penalty, because it it were up to 90% of New Hampshire, they would have put Dickie to death without thinking twice,' Buchanan's lawyer, Mark Sisti, said at this time.

The Justice Center Website reports from the University of Alaska Anchorage for following facts:

- ❖ At the year end of 1997; Florida executed 209 prisoners since 1930. Thirty nine were executed in 1977 and 370 remained under the sentence of death.
- ❖ At the year end of 1997; California executed 296 prisoners since 1930 of whom 4 were executed since 1977, 486 remain under the death sentence.
- ❖ At the year end of 1997; Illinois executed 100 prisoners since 1930 of whom 10 were executed, since 1977, 159 remain under the death sentence.
- ❖ At the year end of 1997; Maryland had executed 70 prisoners since 1930 of whom 2 were executed since 1977; 17 remain under the death sentence.
- ❖ At the year end of 1997; North Carolina executed 271 prisoners since 1930 of whom 8 were executed in 1977, 176 remain under the death sentence.
- ❖ At the year end of 1997 South Carolina has executed 175 prisoners since 1930 of whom 13 were executed since 1977; 68 remain under the death sentence.
- ❖ At the year end of 1997, Washington State had executed 49 prisoners since 1930 of whom 2 were executed in 1977; 12 remain under the death sentence.

- ❖ According to the Lewiston Daily Journal of Friday, June 23, 2000, George W. Bush acknowledges during his 5½ years in office 133 men including women have been executed at Texas Death Row.
(Update on these states according to ProsCon.org updated 3-24-2021 are as follows –)
- ❖ "Florida as of March 13, 2017, Governor Rick Scott signed a bill requesting unanimous death penalty recommendation from a jury and from a judge to impose a sentence."
- ❖ California as of "March 13, 2019, Governor Garvin Newsom issued a memorandum on the death penalty, effective for the duration of his term. He gave temporary reprieves to all 737 death row inmates and closed the execution chamber at San Quentin Prison and stopped states effort to create a constionional lethal injection method."
- ❖ Illinois- "Governor Quinn signed legislation to abolish the death penalty on Mar. 9, 2011."
- ❖ Maryland – "Governor O'Malley signed legislation to abolish the death penalty on May 2, 2013."
- ❖ North Carolina "the death penalty was reinstated in 1977."
- ❖ South Carolina "Capital punishment was reinstated in 1974"
- ❖ Texas "has carried out the most executions in the United States with 483 executions since July 16, 2012."
- ❖ Washinton State "On October 11, 2018 the Supreme Court struck down Washinton's death penalty finding its use was arbitrary and racially discriminatory."

States Have the Death Penalty

Alabama, Arizona, Arkansas, Florida, Georgia, Idaho, Indiana, Kansas, Kentucky, Louisiana, Mississippi, Missouri, Montana, Nebraska, Nevada, North Carolina, Ohio, Oklahoma, South Carolina, South Dakota, Tennessee, Texas, Utah, Wyoming

States and DC Have Abolished the Death Penalty

Alaska, Colorado, Connecticut, Delaware, DC, Hawaii, Illinois, Iowa, Maine, Maryland, Massachusetts, Michigan, Minnesota, New Hampshire, New Jersey, New Mexico, New York, North Dakota, Rhode Island, Vermont, Virginia, Washington, West Virginia, Wisconsin

States Have a Moratorium on the Death Penalty

California, Oregon, Pennsylvania

> *"By the tender mercies of our God, the dawn from on high will break upon us, to give light to those who sit in darkness and in the shadow of death, to guide our feet into the way of peace." (Luke 1:78-79 NRSV)*

Methods of Execution:

Lethal Injection: As of the year end 1996 execution by Lethal Injection was authorized by statute in 32 states.

Electrocution: As of year end 1996 execution by electrocution was authoized by 11 states.

Lethal Gas: As of year end 1996, execution by lethal gas (gas chamber) was authorized by statute in 7 states. (North Carolina also uses lethal injection and electric chair but gas chamber is the primary method).

Hanging: As of year end 1996 execution by hanging was authorized by statute in 4 states. (Washington State also used Lethal injection but hanging was their primary method).

Firing Squad: As of year end 1996 execution by firing squad was authorized by statute in 3 states. {Lethal injection has been authorized in Utah, but the firing squad was the primary method).

"The controversy over the methods of the execution as to some being cruel and unusual punishment which is a violation of the 8th Amendment of the U.S. Constitution."

Joyce A. Leonard

Drawing by unknown Death Row Inmate

Bobby Ray Hopkins of Huntsville, Texas was born on February 23, 1967. He was executed by Lethal Injection on February 12, 2004. He was 36 years old. He spent seven years on death row.

He has an unknown grave.

It may be unknown to the human race, but God marks every grave and knows where they are resting waiting for His return.

As I have entered the articles written by Bobby during the time we spent writing and placing his articles in "Freedom Within' I have once again been disturbed by his death. Perhaps for several reasons. First, he has the same date for his birthday as I do – February 23. Second, he was born the same year as my oldest child 1967. And third, Bobby came to know Jesus while I was writing to him. Then despite the lurid and graphic description of the crime he is said to have committed, he maintained his innocence. I know as I researched his story and even spoke with the journalist that covered his story. There was a doubt that he was the very one who committed these crimes of murder. There were other Bobby Ray Hopkins in the Huntsville, Texas area and he happened to be the poorest, making the act of stealing easier to believe as well as a black man in a state where racism is prevalent. He worked at a well known gas station as an attendant and seemed to do his job well, and was liked by his employer. Those details are not written up in his legacy that detailed his identity and portraying the criminal act whether completely accurate or not it left him as a heinous killer. He had a mother that prayed for him, well known in the community and respected and a sister that cared about him. I wrote to both of them. I am not Bobby's judge nor do I condemn him. Only God knows the actual account and as long as Bobby was honest with God and repented of his sins, he will be in the kingdom. There will be "home sweet home" forever more. Just before his execution he asked if I would be there because he wanted to know someone was there that cared about him. I couldn't. I couldn't bear to watch such a crime even for a crime whether committed or alledgedly committed. It didn't matter. Such a crime would have haunted my memory forever and now all these years later, the impact of his life still is deep within me and my tears are for those who do not know Jesus and continue to cry out "crucify Him" for God is very close to those who He has forgiven and died unashamedly. Bobby will be vindicated in that Day.

Mumia Abu-Jarmal

Who is Mumia Abu-Jarmal? He is a journalist in Pennsylvania who won the Major Armstrong Award for radio journalism. He was named out of Philadelphis'a 'people watch' in 1981 by Philadelphia magazine and he was elected president of the Association of Black Journalism in Philadelphia.

Jarmal exposed police violence against the minority communities in Philadelphia. Even the U.S Department of Justice used the Philadelphia police department to end their brutality and corruption. Beginning when he was 15 years old, the FBI and the

Philadelphia police amassed hundreds of pages of surveillance files on Jarmal for his opposition to racism and police brutality.

In 1982, Jarmal was sentenced to death for the shooting of a police officer. Since then, court hearings have exposed the false evidence and unjust trial that convicted him.

For seventeen years, Jarmal was locked up 23 hours a day and denied contact visits with his family. His confidential legal mail had been opened and reproduced by prison authorities. He was placed in punitive detention for writing his book, 'Live from Death Row.' The U.S. Court Appeals found this punishment to be unconstitutional. The court found the prison officials and guards had yielded to pressure from the Fraternal Order of Police. However journalists are still prohibited from filming or recording interviews with him. Jarmal's appeal for a new trial was won. The support of people around the world including Archbishop Desmond Tutu Nelson Mandela, the European Parlimount, Alice Walker, Paul Newman, Maya Angelou, Sister Helen Prejean, Danny Glover and thousands more.

On October 29, 1998, the Pennsylvania Supreme Court denied Jarmal's appeal for a new trial. His lawyers have appealed this decision.

Elements of an Unfair Trial

- **_The Judge,_** Albert Sabo sentenced more people to death than any other judge in the United States. Six former Philadelphia prosecutors have sworn in court that no accused person could receive a fair trial in Sabo's court room. (Noted that since this act The Public Defender at that time had presided over 30 cases that were convicted and given the death penalty in PA. He died in 2002 at the age of 81)
- **_The Public Defender_**: didn't interview a single witness in the preparation for the 1982 trial, didn't have funds for defending a capital case and informed the court in advance that he wasn't prepared." (Attorney Anthony Jackson)
- "**_The Prosecutor_** used the fact that Mumia at age 15 had been a member of the Black Panther Party as an argument

for imposing the death penalty. This practice was later condemned on unconstitutional by U.S. Supreme Court. The prosecutor removed 11 qualified African Americans from the jury." (Chief Prosecutor Joseph J. McGill still practicing Law in his own law firm).

- ***The Racial Bias*** of Philadelphia's court has resulted in 122 people on death row, all but 113 of them are non-white."

Still after conviction and then being overturned, "a jury delivered a unanimous guilty verdict. Abu-Jarmal was sentenced to death, and though he maintains his innocence and his death sentence was dismissed in 2011, he has remained in prison for the last four decades." He is still awaiting a new trial for a new sentencing.

Quote: October 31, 1994 ~ Mumia Abu-Jarmal "…I remain innocent. A court cannot make an innocent man guilty. Any ruling founded on injustice is not justice. The righteous fight for life, liberty and for justice can only continue." (Disclaimer: This article is not necessarily the opinion of the author or of "Freedom Within" when the article was sent to "Freedom Within" as written, however, we believed then as I believe still in freedom of speech and freedom of the pen.)

Joyce A. Leonard

"Hell on Earth"

"Gloomy place of defeat,
It's cold gray walls, a wasting sheet,
Massive warehouse of despair,
Loneliness is nurtured there.
Grimy edifice of decay
Where social conscience rots away;
Dismal structure of disgrace,
Where mankind hides his other face.
Angry hearts, hatred fired,
Where criminality is inspired;
Putrid playground of perversion,
Sad, dispicable, sick diversion,
An ugly monument to ugly souls.
Hatred driven toward ugly goals.
A cold gray womb if shameful deeds
Are fertilized by hatred's seeds.
Tragic fortress walls of time,
Built by fear to combat crime.
A waiting pace of human lives,
Where blatent evil revives,
A brewing sac of all that is vile,
Spewing out its social bile.
A rampant midevil thought
That men are cleansed as they rot!
In the catacombs of lonely cages,
An ignorant throwback of the dark ages.
Hideous error of our time
In itself a monstrous crime;
Grim dark shadows of our lands,
This is where the prison stands."

By Kevin Tardiff – (MSP – 1998)

Out of the Darkness... "Freedom Within"

By Stan Wetmore 1998

> # ~Attention~
> # *Public Hearing*

CHAPTER SEVEN

"**On** March 17, 1997 in a routine traffic stop by State Police, a warrant was discovered for the arrest of Gerald H. LeBlanc for 1978 violation of parole. He was returned to prison.

The following is the verbatim finding of the April 3,1997 - Parole Board Hearing: 'You told the Parole Board that you thought Governor Longley did away with parole, and that because of the change you were no longer required to report to the Parole Officer.

On June 1, 1979, the California Parole authorities reported that your whereabouts were unknown and they terminated supervision of your case. A warrant was issued on June 21, 1978 and you were arrested on that warrant in 1997. Prior to being granted this Parole, you had gone to California without permission.'

'Based on the seriousness of your crime and the fact that you absconded from supervision in 1978, the Parole Board voted to to deny you 10 years flat from April 3, 1997.'

No consideration that a verifiable work history from release in 1972, until my retirement exist were considered. The arresting State Police officer was made, and was given the information by me so as to make a complete background check. The prison also has that information.

Twenty-four years ago the inherent inequalities and unfairnesss of the mandatory life sentence was corrected. A new stataue imposing sentence according to the degree of culpability was made.

All sentences are subject to review to correct and adjust, unfair sentence except the old mandatory life sentence, which can only be reviewed and corrected by executive action, that is by the Govenor, himself.

I submitted a petition to have my sentence commuted to those commensurate with the new statute. The Commutation Board denied me a hearing, the reason was circumstances not exceptional the fact the Legislature regarded the statute unjust, unfair is not exceptional?!

The statement of both witnesses 'shooting accidental' in their opinion (the brother of the victim). The fact the court records, 'Newspaper report (APP 6/17/1958) shows I didn't fire the shot. The fact to be considered is imposing a just sentence truly clemency or it is righting a wrong?

And who makes up the board called the Governor's Board of Executive Clemency?

The Governor's Board of Executive Clemency is comprised of three, (3) attorney's who if, I believe were representing me, would certainly consider that an inequitable sentence were more than sufficient reasons in commute to one that was just.

Are wealth and influence the only circumstances that are exceptional? Twenty-four years ago (at this writing 1999) under Governor Longley, the Legislature abolished Parole, as being unfair and subject to the personal whims and prejudice of those who managed the system.

Since that time a number of inmates eligible for Parole has decreased until only a very few remain, and by Executive Action (commutation) can and should remove the ependiture of tax money from a system deemed unfair etc.

In stating these facts and opinions, I do not imply that a fair and just Parole system is not needed. On the contrary, it is absolutely needed. Properly administered by competent personnel. Parole is a valuable way in returning the offender back into society at the optimum time of rehabilitation, and while the positive effects of prison exert an influence on his personality, such as being unhappy and discontented, the feeling of helplessness and despair, Parole offers hope, giving incentive to self-evaluate, to reflect on past errors, and plan a future, and many more reasons exist.

By all means a new and fair Parole system should be established. Otherwise, the major industry in Maine will be building, staffing and maintainng of prisons without voter approval.

In closing, I shall never, ever acquience in being denied a fair hearing to correct an obvious wrong with words 'Circimstances not exceptional.'

So because the Board has thwarted my attempt to petition the Governor, I petition you, the citizens where the ultimate power and authority resides."

    (Submitted and written by Gerald H. LeBlanc MSP – 1999)

Inside and Out

CHAPTER EIGHT

This segment was written and submitted by an inmate at Maine State Prison in 1999 annonymously

Police Procedures

"It is common practice of law enforcement agencies to seize on a piece of evidence that leads them to believe that a certain suspect is the guilty party. When contradictory evidence appears, they ignore it, unwilling to believe that their original belief was false, and the longer the orignal belief is held the more difficult it becomes to shift. When no corroborative evidence appears to reinforce the belief, it has to be manufactured – not with objective or framing an innocent person, but as the police believe of bringing a guilty one to justice.

There are various ways in which evidence is manufactured crudely by planting things or forging incriminating documents more subtly by persuading witnesses to give erronous testimony against a suspect. To this, the police employ highly effective methods. Several policemen together (for there is strength in numbers) tell the witness that they have got the right person, and there is not the slightest doubt about it, and all they want the witness to do is say that he or she saw the suspect where and whenever the police say they did.

Inside and Out - Police Procedures

The witness is flattered to think that his/her opinion is of such importance and they believe the police know far more about the case than he/she does, and as a law abiding citizen he or she has no wish to obstruct the course of justice.

So the witness agrees, if not at the first time of asking, usually (as police are tenatious) at the second or third, then having commited themselves on an untruth, they and everyone else come to believe in it. If he/she doesn't comply, the police chameleon – can become hostile and threatening, sporting an attitude that says, "If you don't want to cooperate with us we can make things tough for you, very tough indeed."

Life in Maximum Security – Super Max

The living conditions at MCI are divided into two units known as B-side and C-side, which is also known as Hard Side and Soft Side. There are 50 cells on each side. The cells are 7 feet X 12 ft and have solid steel doors, except for a vision window for the guards and a tray slot that is always kept locked. There are two stainless steel tables connected to the walls, a stainless steel sink, and toilet built together in one unit. There is an overhead florescent light with a night light built into it, which stays on constantly. The overhead light is able to be put on and off by the prisoner. There is a window that is three and a half feet tall and three inches wide, which gives limited view of the outside.

The beds are made of concrete with two and a half inch mattress pad. There are three storage sections under the beds. There are square holes in all four corners of the bed that are made for a device that will keep prisoners strapped down. As of June 1, 1999, this device has not been put into use as MCI has and uses three retraint chairs (known as the 'black chair) on prisoners. Should a prisoner promote problems, they would be secured in that 'black chair.' Then the prisoner would be mace sprayed, stripped down and mace used again. Prisoners remain unwashed after this procedure while in these black chairs as the chemicals have a burning sensation. The secretion of body perspiration reactivates the chemicals causing the prisoner to remain in extreme pain.

In 1998 the Maine Department of Corrections was taken to court for this abusive behavior toward a prisoner with the use of one of their chairs. A guard had strapped a towel around the head of a prisoner, causing him to loose consciousness, and yet these chairs remain in use as a tactic of abusive control even after loosing their court case.

The Boldoc Correctional Facility provides the food that is served at the Maine State Prison as well as the MCI. Food is brought into the prison in bulk, placed on trays, and transferred to a cart that keeps the food either hot or cold. Often the food is held up to 45 minutes before being served to the inmates in their cells.

There are two religious group services provided. Approximately once or twice a month an inmate may or may not have the priviledge of seeing the chaplain if he is available.

Prisoners are allowed to recieve up to three one hour visits a week that are non-contact only. Prisoners are brought to visitations booths handcuffed and removed once inside the booth. Prisoners and visitors are seperated by concrete as well as two thick Plexiglas windows. Conversations are held by phone for monitoring purposes. Special management Unit. (SMU) prisoners are brought to visitation booths in four point shackles and have to remain that way during the confined visit.

All prisoners on B-Side are subjected to a strip search before they leave their cells. Should you refuse to comply with their demands, you could loose whatever privilege you were going to (recreation/visit/etc.) or receive a write up for refusing to obey an order.

Prisoners are allowed out of their cells five times a week for one hour recreation which is spent within an approximate five feet by 20 foot dog run, outside regardless of weather conditions. There are no inside recreation areas. Within view of the prisoner is another dog run for police canine that have water, food and shelter provided.

Showers are allowed for a fifteen minute period, three times a week, which is part of their one hour recreation time. Those confined to C-side have an inside day room or outside 'bull pen' and or both. They are able to have a two-hour Rec time. Within the 'bull-pen' there is a parallel bar, basketball hoop that provides exercise. Those from SMU on B-side are able to have Rec inside an empty concrete yard with 25 ft. high walls, enclosed by razor wire at the top and shackled with 4-point restraints during their Rec time.

B-side prisoners are allowd to make three 15 minute phone calls a week on a phone brought to them by the guard via the food slot to the door. If you do not reach the person you are trying to call, more often than not you will not get another chance or you will have to wait until the next designated phone day. Prisoners on 'disciplinary time' are not allowed to use the phone. Prisoners on C-side are allowed to make as many phone calls as they want to during their 2-hour Rec time, seven days a week.

Shaving privileges are allowed on B-side twice a week and once a week for SMU, but everyday for C-side prisoners.

The most trivial of violations are enforced as prisoners are not able to violate high class violations other than verbal threatening or feces slinging, since there is no contact with each other while on B-side. On C-side the only other violation may be physical fighting during Rec time.

Incident reports, known as 'write-ups' as well as Informal Resolutions are given when a violation is committed by a prisoner. An Informal resolution is a way for a prisoner who has been caught in a violation to avoid a 'write-up.' The guard has the right to offer the prisioner up to seven days loss of their recreation and or phone priviledges.

Prisoners will be allowed to take showers during the days they have received the Informational Resolution. This procedure is good for the prisoner in many ways and it is offered most of the time because it saves the guards from doing a report. Prisoners rather handle their violations in this way as they know they would be found guilty and lose more by getting through their procedure accompanied by the fact that write-ups can be used against them while waiting for approval to enter the general population at Maine State Prison.

Each time a prisoner on B-side leaves his cell, a guard will search the cell for 'contraband' by turning all the belongings in the cell upside down. Should you leave your cell as often as three times in a day, it is done each time, even if it is known that there is no known contraband within that cell from the previous search.

Prisoners are allowed three general reading books from the library a week, and five law books twice a week. Those in SMU are allowed only one general reading book a week and one law book twice a week. Those who are on 'diciplinary time are not allowed anythng to read unless after 90, days being write-up free for thirty days, only then can a prisoners be approved to read books.

C-side prisoners are able to earn one day good -time and be able to work. This unit is the next step into release into general population at the main prison. Those approved to be transferred have waited any where from 9 months to years before their final transfer. There are some who have never received a write-up and still they have not been approved to be released to the general population.

On B-side there are three units in one. There are 15 cells that house the Administrative and Disciplinary units of the of the prison. Also before money was approved by Maine's taxpayers, the Maine Department of Corrections lied without hesitation to the taxpayers of Maine that MCI needed to be built to hold 'Maine's 100 Most Dangerous Prisoners,' and within five years after being built, and opened, the prisoners were housed at MCI as well as protective custody prisoners. It was known that MCI would never hold 100 dangerous prisoners from the very start!

B-side also holds ten cells for the Special Management Unit. (SMU) These prisoners are listed as being a potential threat to MCI and/or others as well as themselves. Two of these cells have cameras and speakers built into them to monitor the prisoner at all times. Guards are able to talk with and/or listen in these two cells. These are the most incomprehensible units at MCI. The prisoners in these units cannot come out of their cells without a sargeant present and with a four-point restraints which is being handcuffed, then shackled and then another set of shackles connected between the first two, The prisoner must remain in this four-point restraint at all times out of their cells with the exception of showering, but not going to and from the shower.

The feeding procedure for SMU is to request that the prisoner stand at the back of the wall in their cell while the guard throws a paper bag in the cell either at the prisoner or on the floor. The bag usually contains two sandwiches of peanut butter with no jelly or three slices of cheese with mustard, a few raw vegetables, one cut up fruit and no drink. This meal is served the same for all three meals each day for the duration of the prisoners stay at SMU.

The remaining 25 cells on B-side serve as 'Hard Side,' and a little less restrictive than SMU, When leaving their cell for whatever reason, they are escorted by two guards as well as being handcuffed behind their back and/or having the use of the four-point shackles.

The justice that demands payment for a crime within certain institutions desensitizes and breeds inhuman tactics that demoralize, seething with hatred rather than rehabilitating the mind to rejoin society one day contributing to the abiding function of the community."

>(Taken from Volume 3 Issue 1 from "Freedom Within" 2000 -
>Written and submitted by Kevin Tardiff – Maine State Prison)

It was noted by the Newsletter "Freedom Within" that we did not intend to criticize the guards at MCI. They had always maintained a professional and respectful reception toward us as a Prison Ministry Outreach and we encouraged any responses and comments from them in order to maintain a fair balance. There were no recipients that came through with this challenge.

"Incarceration Rates"

Something to think about...

The United States holds the highest incarceration rate per capita in the world. There is currently 1.8 million men and women behind bars and an estimated 3.9 million on probation and parole, thus putting the total for the entire criminal justice/correctional population within the country at appproximatley 3-7 individuals.

There is also to date (year 2000) 1,500 more men and women being added to the system weekly, and at this rate in the year 2050, almost half of the American population will be behind bars for some type of criminal offense.

It is interesting to also note that there are 1.4 million children today with imprisoned parents and there are 5 million immediate family members with relatives currently incarcerated, this leaving an enormous void within each family.

While men do commit most of the crime in this country, there has been drastic increase in the number of women being incarcerated over the past decade.

Women are now the new and fast rising statistic within the U.S. penal system, with currently more than 80,000 women in prison, 650,000 on probation and 79,000 on parole as compared to 1990 when women represented less than 25% of the criminal justice system."

(Article submitted annonmously from Maine State Prison.)

"The statistics are since 2000 the world's prison population has matched the growth of the overall population, increasing by 24%, according to the World Prison Brief (WPB), an online database hosted by the Institute for Criminal Policy Research at the University of London. Yet just five countries account for slightly more than half of the world's estimated 10.75 million people being held in penal institutions: the U.S., China, Brazil, Russia and India." This is according to Google research.

"The Love of God"

The "Love of God," which was written by Frederick M. Lehman in 1917.

The verse he found etched on the walls of a prison asylum go like this:
"Could we with ink the ocean fill, and were
the skies of parchment made;
Were every stalk on earth a quill, and every man a scribe by trade.
To write the love of God above, would drain the ocean dry;
Nor could the scroll contain the whole, though stretched from sky to sky"

Memorials

*"It is far better to light the candle
than curse the darkness"
By William L. Watkinson 1907*

CHAPTER NINE

On the following pages I would like to make tribute to those I came to know, during the time in Prison Ministry. They became friends to our ministry and one day we will know how their hearts were touched during the five short years we spent with them in letter and visits.

Paul E. Fortin II, 35, of Lewiston, Maine died November 25, 1999.

He had begun a new life outside of the prison walls and was doing very well. He was working and was determined to show his family that he was trustworthy and responsible. He was killed in a hit and run incident. He had attended school in Mechanic Falls, ME during his elementary years. He was well known in the community.

BETTY BEETS was executed in Texas 02/24/2000.

"Zero Days to Live for Betty Beets"
by Pajama Lady 02/06/2000

"The clock is ticking loud and fast,
Yesterday is already today.
Betty is more than her past,
Time rolled old sins away.
Texans will place her beneath the sod.
Betty knows the day, the hour,
She's a new creature in God.
While the executioner drools in his power,
But Betty with dignity can leave.
While the killer hides his face,
And I will grieve, and I'll grieve, and I'll grieve, and I'll grieve,
For the Texas national disgrace.
Though this lady with unblemished soul,
Can surely make use of the rest.
I am certain that when they call the roll,
Betty will be with the best.
But those of you with nothing to say,
You will have to account for that,
For you may be in Betty's shoes one day,
And what do you think of that?"

LARRY ROBISON – Mentally Ill and was executed January 21, 2000 in Texas. His story aired on 48 Hours January 13, 2000, His mother, Lois Robison wrote the essay "Why Our Mentally Ill Son is on Texas Death Row. George W. Bush ignored the plea to stop this execution and Texas ignored the international outcry.

DENNIS LARSON: Dennis was quick wit and humorous. I personally wrote to him and sent used postage stamps to his mother as she had a massive stamp collection. Dennis' death was a suicide there at Maine State Prison. I received shortly after his death some mail concerning some protocol within the prison that could be damaging. He had instructed that it be mailed to me at the event of his death. It was sent and I received it. Dennis is free at last for he was facing extradition to his home state and execution. He did not want his mother to endure that heartache.

The window pane that has lost its view and becomes the window of pain that only Jesus can renew. Artwork by Inmate David Jack Federal Inmate

BEN LAFARRIER – known as Big Ben died 08/19/2001 at South Windham Correctional Center. He was a man who loved God and enjoyed having the Bible read to him. He could not see, but he saw through the eyes of others and loved to reminisce about his times in the Maine woods. He had once enjoyed the great outdoors. Ben was a friend to those who knew him and took the time to get to know him.

DEAN CURTIS – Died the fall of 2000 – He loved to sing and had an exceptional tenor voice. He also wrote songs. He wrote the following poem in May 1994:

> "In my cell I wonder why,
> I know the things I have done are bad.
> I try so hard though not to cry,
> To put away the life I had.
> I know I will never leave alive.
> Yet, sorrow does not fill my soul.
> Inside of me all hopes thrive.
> I know I can reach my goal,

I have found a Friend, Who has great love,
Though I cannot yet see His face.
Someday I will live with Him above,
And bask within His awesome grace.
I am afraid no more to die,
I know that time will quickly pass,
Then I will be up in the sky,
With my dear Lord, happy at last."

Drawing by Stan Wetmore former inmate at MSP

"Life is No Joke"

"When I was young, everything was a joke to me.
I didn't know what would come of it, I couldn't see.
I saw people working and dreaming,
I was the one hustling and scheming.
I was just a kid.
I never thought I would be facing a 25-year bid.
I used to think I knew it all,
Little did I know I was setting myself up for a fall.
I always had to be in the spotlight,
And everybody was wrong, and I was right.
I chose the wrong path for a long time –
That path was drugs and alcohol which led to crime.
There were times I would do right,
But I always turned back to drugs with little fight.

Joyce A. Leonard

I was partying and having a blast.
I didn't see I was going nowhere fast.
My goal was to have more fun every day,
Now I know fun doesn't always pay.
Drugs always took me down the scale.
The final number was always jail.
I never thought I would get caught,
But here I am in prison to rot.
Drugs took it all away from me.
It even took my right to live free.
I am sorry Mom & Dad, I made you sad.
You showed me good, and I was bad.
I would always just do
And never think of what I put you through.
Today I think of all the people I have hurt;
It makes me sad; I feel like dirt.
Everything went by so fast –
I wish I could go back and change the past.
To all those who are young and still have a chance,
Try your hardest and you shall advance."

By Christopher "Brownie" Brown

Christopher requested in a suicide note that this poem be printed in as many papers it could be to save others before they get into trouble. He hung himself in the New Hampshire State Prison – July 6, 1998

Robert "Paco" Alan Pazant July 7, 1967 – January 6, 2023

I first came to know Paco as we affectionately called him at Maine State Prison where he spent a good part of his life. He made a tremendous turn around by becoming an advocate in the prison hospice program. "He considered it a privilege to care for a man in hospice knowing that he himself would not want to die alone.' He joined the Maine Prisoner Advocacy Coalition as a coordinator in 2020 to continue his work with inmates.

He showed up at my door in the summer of 2022. We reconnected. He had a fantastic voice and wrote a song putting it to music with his guitar. The week before he was killed in a head on crash, he had given me a hug in my garage and told me he loved me. He called me 'Ma.' He called my son 'Bro' and they too had connected. My heart grieved over him. Ironically, he died alone at that collision. He left a father, three brothers and seven sisters as well as many who came to know him loved him.

***Grieving Thoughts in Prayer*–** This is where the prayer ends. The enemy took one of Your boys to their destiny. You allowed it just as you have others I have loved. The sanctity of life has been taken. A time taken from someone. The ending of one life, the beginning of another. The last memory stays embedded and is never lost. The sting of death for an unsaved soul is the devil's glee. It takes its toll. I am not the judge. Thank you, Lord for sparing human minds with making unjust decisions. Your mercies are new, given and reproduced each day. Where this brother was in mixed emotions – I only speculate, but maybe I will see him again in that Day. Amen

ALBERT PAUL

Albert Paul – died at the age of 87 at the Mountain View Correctional Center in Maine on March 15, 2021. It is said it was from COVID 19 related issues. He is the oldest inmate to have died in the Maine State Prison.

I corresponded with Al during the time I was in Prison Ministry. He was an interesting man. He had committed many robberies and was in the system most of his life starting at age 18. In 1971 he was convicted of murder and sentenced to life in prison. He had escaped three times from prison and once for only 24 hours then turned himself in. Most of his time at Maine State Prison was in solitary since he was considered an escape artist.

Penned from Joyce in "Freedom Within" Newsletters

CHAPTER TEN

> *"The Spirit of the Lord God is upon Me,*
> *Because the Lord has anointed Me*
> *To preach good tidings to the poor;*
> *He has sent Me to heal the broken hearted,*
> *To proclaim liberty to the captives,*
> *And the opening of the prison to those who are bound;*
> *(Isaiah 61:1) NKJV*

Luke 19:1-19 tells the story of the 'Zacchaeus principle.' Rather than telling you what it is, I want you to read it for yourselves In the Gospel of Luke. Zacchaeus went looking for Jesus, and he was not disappointed. He found a way above the press of the crowd to see Him.

You will not be disappointed as you find a way to escape the pressures of your daily life and look for Jesus in the quietness of your time spent in solitude, relinquishing to Him and persevering in thankfulness that draws power developed from the faith of a grain of mustard seed. The necessity of this relationship will produce victories for the unspoken prayers that were once a wish. The unanswered prayers will become the answer as we Xerox our lives after the Creator and follow the Zacchaeus principle.

Joyce A. Leonard

"Search for Me with all Your Heart"

Sometimes it is difficult to make heads
or tails of what life has to give,
We reason the pros and cons and weigh
the balance of the life we live.
We forget to inhale the breath of life,
Being filled with anger and aiding the breath of strife.
Calm is needed for the raging answers of my mind,
Where intense criticism is all, I find.
I need Thy precious assurance of peace,
That Thy precious promises will never cease.
I beg that evil will not have its way with me.
Rebuke the echoes of its curse and set me free.
'Child, search for Me with all your heart,
I will calm your fears and thwart the flying dart.
Don't let go of the loveliness within your fingertips,
Don't cast aside the blessing from My lips.
I have spoken your name when you searched for Me
Beside the tangled mass and beside the stump of the tree.
I was there when you could not see.
I heard your cries, and the flower you dropped was Me.'
Forgive me Lord for the anger I dispelled,
For the doubt and fears that I held.
I thought I had already searched Thee out,
But in a few moments, I let my faith turn to doubt.
Thank you, Lord, for being in control when I was lost.
For buying me back at ransoms cost.
Remind me again when mistrusting begins to start
To search for Thee once more with all of my heart.'

Have you ever lost a loved one so dear to you that it was difficult to get over that pain of that loss? Perhaps that person had been so close to you that there were reminders at every turn that brought them back to your mind and then the grieving process would begin again. Have you ever said, "I would give my right arm" to have that loved one back in my life again? Perhaps there was something you neglected to tell them…maybe how much they meant to you. Perhaps you didn't tell them you were sorry for any pain you may have caused them. There are many reasons.

Being separated from a positive force in your life is painful, whether it is physical separation or that of a mental, emotional as well as spiritual nature.

Jesus is called the "Vine" in John 15. As long as we stay connected to the Vine, there is life in every aspect even in the "dark days." And Jesus says in John 15:13, "Greater love hath no man than to lay down his life for his friends."

Well, I'd' give my right arm, but my life? Could you take the lethal injection for your friend on death row? Could you stand in the balance of death and let your friend go free? Tough question. Jesus did that. He stood between you and death. He defeated the enemy so that you and I could have eternal life. Yet, there are many of us whether we are inside prison walls or outside in our own created prison walls, serving what is called a" jailhouse religion." Many play games with God as well as with those who are reaching out to them. They wear one hat for religion and another hat for the world.

Yet, the Vine, our Savior accepts us where we are, and nurtures us in the crisis. When things get better, human nature takes back the selfish attitude and puts our Friend on the back burner tending to forget who gave them the endurance to endure.

Jesus laid down His life for His friends. Those who accept Him, He calls friends. He doesn't throw that title away because we walk away from Him. He waits. At every turn there is a reminder of the separation. Life itself is a reminder.

Service of gratitude is a debt we must pay giving it with joy for that friendship with the "Living Vine." To give without joy isn't giving! Who wants a gift if it is given with a curse under your breath or a frown on your face or the look of disdain in your eye? "Every man according as he purposes in his heart, so let him give, not grudgingly, or of necessity; for God loves a cheerful giver." (II Corinthians 9:7) I believe giving goes beyond the financial increase into the increase of love for the brethren. Whatever you put your hand to do, do it with all your might in service to the Lord for his debt of friendship to you.

"*Whatever your hand finds to do, do it with all your might, for in the grave where you are going, there is neither working or planning, nor knowledge nor wisdom.*" (Ecclesiastes 9:10 NIV) If you separate yourself from Him when the road seems easy, you are serving the religion of a fool and walking away from the greatest friend you will ever have.

"Flowering... Fading... Friendships"

"The fragrant flocks growing tall,
As the summer scene ends in Fall.
The delicate beauty of a rose that blooms,
Yet the loveliness of flowers always fades.
But when at last, we reach heaven our hopes will be stayed.
We think of changes heaven has for us;
No sadness, broken dreams, or fleshly lusts.
No tears filled with sorrows or fading flowers,
Our imaginations cannot soar in all its powers
To ever extend to what Jesus has in store,
Will be beyond our wildest dreams and more,
It's not just the flowers that fade here on earth.
It's the closeness of friendships and the parting of mirth.
Locked in the arms that once held each other in intimate thought,
Memories of friendships faded by the tempter's knot.
In heaven these friendships will never die.
Sadness of their loss won't make me cry.
Daffodils display their sunny heads,
Gladiolas of white, pink, and flaming reds,
Die when plucked within a short while-
But heaven will hold these beauties on brilliant style…
And friendships will last forever,
And love for each other will die never,"

(Written by Joyce A. Leonard 08-16-1992)

"You are Invited"

Penned from Joyce *- (Parable paraphrased from Luke 14:15-24)*

The invitation was embossed with gold lettering, and it was sent to me!

I was invited to attend the wedding feast of the Governor. It was to be held at the Governor's mansion. I was so excited to be part of the chosen few to attend this event. The event of the year!

I called my friends that I knew that were named on the invitation list. "What are you going to wear to the festivities?" I asked. "Wear?" was the reply. "I'm not going to be part of that hob-knobbing with all the snobs. He didn't do me any favors by asking me.

Saddened by their denial to join the event, I called another friend I knew. "Aren't you excited that we were asked to come to the Governor's wedding festival? Can you believe it?" I was dancing with enthusiasm. But the reply quickly caused my sparkle to dim. "I have prior plans, so I am not going. I don't know what makes him think I would just drop everything to put him first."

I couldn't believe my friend would act this way, but as I looked at the list, I recognized another name, so I called them for surely, they would go.

"No, I don't know that many that will be there, and I will feel uncomfortable around those strange people. Besides those that are going are just going for show. They are a bunch of hypocrites, and I don't want to be around them."

The day of the event arrived, and I wanted to be ready to be a part of every aspect of it so I prepared myself early and was the first one there. It took my breath away as I admired the crystal chandeliers hanging over the tables draped with the purest white linen, and shining silver nestled next to the China sparkling in the lighting.

The fragrance of roses entwined with daffodils mingled with the colors of the snap dragons, spotted with baby's breath gracing the mantels as well as every door casing which was so lovely that words failed my comprehension that this was real.

The Governor came in to make sure all was in order before everything was to begin. He caught sight of me gasping at the beauty and asked where my friends were. I told him as gently as I could and extended my apologies. I saw a tear glisten in the corner of his eye, then he became angry. He gave me the money to go quickly to the prisons and bring back as many of the prisoners that could be released. He would make the necessary phone calls and then to go to the ghetto of the city and call everyone there that was hungry to 'come.' But not to stop there, go to the hospitals where the sick and the dying lay in depression and bring them to fill the hours and moments of their lives with happiness. For, he said, "I want my halls to be filled with those who want to be fed and filled with laughter, with joy, with happiness and love that they will taste what I have prepared for them."

> *"Today, I must abide at your house," so the word will come to them, and those who are supposed to be hardened sinners will be found to have hearts as tender as a child's because Christ has deigned to notice them. Many will come from the grossest error and sin and will take the place of others who have had opportunities and privileges but have not prized them. They will be accounted the chosen of God, elect, precious, and when Christ shall come into His kingdom, they will stand next to His throne."* ("Christ's Object Lessons" pg. 236 by EG White)

"To Vow or Not to Vow"

Every day is a new beginning. Every day is another day closer to the eminent coming of Jesus Christ. The Bible has set many signs and prophecies before us so we will know that His return is soon, even though we don't know the day or the hour. Many tend to forget that life can be snuffed out from us at any given moment of time, and we never know when that might be! The important question is – 'Are we ready?'

Joshua made a vow unto the Lord in Joshua 24:14 & 15 saying, 'Choose you this day whom you will serve…as for me and my house, we will serve the Lord.' Once a commitment is made in the eyes of God, it is sacred. Moses spoke to the heads of the tribes of Israel concerning this matter, saying, 'This is the thing which the Lord has commanded: 'If a man makes a vow to the Lord, or swears an oath to bind himself by some agreement, he shall not break his word, he shall do all that proceeds out of his mouth.' (Numbers 30:2-3)

The Psalmist wrote in Psalms 76:11 'Make a vow to your Lord God and pay them,' reinforced by Solomon in Ecclesiastes 5:4 & 5 'When you make a vow to God do not delay to pay it, for He has no pleasure in fools.' Pay what you have vowed – better not to vow than to vow and not to pay.' What? Better not to vow than to vow and not pay? Does that mean in other matters other than money? Well, a vow is a vow, right?

The dictionary tells me the meaning of the word 'vow 'is as solemn promise to God; a pledge of faithfulness; to declare assurance to an emphatic affirmance. How often is this pledge taken lightly with an attitude the same as 'rules were made to be broken. 'so, promises too?

NO. That is not the criteria for the Christian, but the backslider, (ooh that is a nasty word) that has taken their vow lightly to serve the Lord to the end, may be thinking, 'but I can jump back on the band wagon anytime.' Maybe so, my friend, but aren't we playing a game with God by doing that? He is not just in this for fun and games.

He vowed once again, that where He is there, we may be also. (John 14:1-3) He vowed to forgive us of our sins and cleanse us from all unrighteousness. (I John 1:9) He vowed to hold our hand in every crisis, open the eyes of the blind and let the prisoners go free. (Isaiah 42:5-9) There are many more vows to follow these promises from our covenant keeping God. He will keep His end of the bargain! So, join me as I pledge, 'as for me and my house, we will serve the Lord.' As we wait with great anticipation for our King, Who is coming. I long to hear His words, 'Well done, thou good and faithful servant.' (Matthew 25:21)

"The Beauty"

The lives that live for our Savior are the diamonds that glitter.
A golden life filled with sweetness outweighs what is bitter.
A gem is carved and chiseled from an ugly gray rock,
With beauty that no other treasure can mock.
The diamond and the life are one and the same.
Both are valued by the cut of the master's ordain.
It is the patience in chiseling that brings out the beauty,
Both in forming and the call to duty.
The greatest value reflects the work of the Master's hand,
A life that glitters like diamonds in the sand."

By Joyce A, Leonard

"The Christian of Love or The Tare of Hypocrisy?"

Some call it human decency while others wave it off as 'human nature.' The Bible tells us in Jeremiah 17:9, 'The heart is deceitful above all things, and desperately wicked, who can know it?' Sad to say that some of these unchristian qualities and bad attitudes appear when 'self' is being served regardless of the nature of the beast! It is only when the heart repents of 'self' that the effectual conversion takes place and the soul becomes the Christian of love, following the Master's footsteps.

Many have tasted the 'kiss of Judas' among our Christian brothers and sisters when they displayed the carnal nature. Compassion, tender heartedness, forgiving one another, peace, self-control and love was just not a part of their vocabulary. They had measured up a little while talking the talk but fell short when it came to walking the walk and turning the other cheek (which by the way gets slapped harder than the first time around) and picking up the cross to follow Jesus.

It seems that somewhere along the line, having to drag that cross becomes a burden of drudgery and not a burden of love for the

Man who never complained, never spoke back a hateful word and never rushed to His own defense.

It was the wickedness of man, the unchristian hypocritical bigot as well as the chosen self-righteous, prideful 'goodie-two-shoes' for whom Christ died. Beloved, it was for you and me, those with the deceitful assumption of virtue, which is the definition of hypocrite. For any good thing that comes from anyone of us, comes not from within ourselves, but by the Spirit of the living God.

You will find at every bend in the road, two classes. The most prominent place to find them is in the church pews. You expect to find them in the world, and the church is supposed to be the 'safe' territory. But Jesus says the wheat and the tares will grow together until He comes. (Matthew 19:24-30) The tares can't be taken out from among the wheat in fear of uprooting and disturbing the wheat so they must stay until the harvest and the harvest is when Jesus returns. Read further in Matthew where Jesus explains the process to us along with His disciples in Matthew 13:36-43.

Does that mean we shouldn't go to church? We see enough of this in the world so why do we have to be a part of it in the church? We are admonished to 'stir up love and good works, not forsaking the assembling of ourselves together as is the manner of some, but exhorting, (encouraging, urging, warning), one another, and so much more as you see the Day approaching." (Hebrews 10:24-25) The 'day' approaching is the 'day' of Jesus return. Which will be, my friend, the Christian of love waiting or the tare of hypocrisy?

"Hoodwinked Again?"

What do you say when the enemy comes into your house and smiles, while looking at you with pleasant eyes and cooing soft words to console? When months, days and even just moments ago you swore within yourself, "I will not forgive, I will not forget...I will not...I will not..."

As a Christian you walk in a path that Jesus walked and taking on that decision to follow Christ even to the cross. You are dragging the tree that He dragged, claiming the death that He died and taking on the responsibility of the unconditional forgiveness…the unconditional agape love.

And Jesus said, *'But I say to you, love your enemies and pray for them who persecute you.'* (Matthew 5:44) So your friendly enemy has looked you in the eye and so not to be caught up in their own lie, knowing you are and advocate for truth, they know you have to forgive because you keep the commandments of God and Jesus said, *'For if you forgive others their trespasses, your heavenly Father will also forgive you; but if you do not forgive others, neither will your heavenly Father forgive you your trespasses.'* (Matthew 6:14 &15)

Sounds like you are caught between a rock and a hard place, and you are. You have been wronged, scourged by the enemy, and have the right to feel the way you do. You are justified to hate. Well, as the world supports this as true, but as the life of a consecrated, converted Christian, it may be another story.

'Bless those who persecute you and do not curse. Rejoice with those who rejoice and weep with those who weep. Be of the same mind toward one another. Do not set your mind on high things but associate with the humble. Do not be wise in your own opinion'

'Repay no one evil for evil. Have regard for good things in the sight of all men. If it is possible as much as it depends on you, live peaceably with all men. Beloved do not avenge yourselves, but rather give place to wrath; for it is written, Vengeance is Mine, I will repay, says the Lord. Therefore, if your enemy is hungry, feed him. If he is thirsty, give him a drink; for in so doing you will heap coals of fire in his head.' (Romans 13:14-20)

Then the Lord gives relief with these words, "*Sit at My right hand until I put your enemies under your feet.*" *(Matthew 22:44)* "*For with God it is a righteous thing to trouble those who give trouble to you.*" (II Thessalonians 1:6)

So, by following the counsel found within the Holy Scriptures and forgiving the incident of the situation, are you setting yourself up to be "hoodwinked again?" Are you giving your enemies more bait to lure you under their articulate deception? Are you allowing them to have the last laugh at your expense? Yes, it is a risk, but God promises that the rewards outweigh the pleasure *of sin and that was what Moses chose. (Read Hebrews 11:25-26)*

"*So, God will bring every good work into judgment including every secret thing, whether good or evil."* (Ecclesiastes 12:14) When Solomon had attained every achievement possible, and held great power with riches of untold degree and came to heights of accomplishment that we rarely even dream about, he testified, "*Then I looked on all the works that my hands had done and the labor in which I toiled; and indeed, all was vanity and grasping for wind. There was no profit under the sun."* (Ecclesiastes 2:11)

So are we expected to set aside these iniquities, injustices, horrors, cruel and obscene deliberate acts done to us at the hand of our enemies and smile back at their evil vicious lies with eyes full of tears and say, 'Yes, I forgive you?' Well, isn't that what Jesus did on the cross when He cried out, *"Father forgive them…"* (Luke 23:34) in a pain we will never fully understand or comprehend?

But my friend, you cannot do this in your own power or strength because it is not in the ability of the carnal human nature to be able to forgive such acts against us, but as you take on the nature of Jesus' character and become transformed by His love…only then will you be able to forgive and separate the sin from the sinner. *"For God so loved the world that He gave His only begotten Son, that whosoever believes in Him should not perish but have everlasting life."* (John 3:16)

"As Time Goes On"

Each of us has the gift of twenty-four hours in a day. To some it can mean boredom and drudgery. Just the passing of time from the beginning to the end of yet another day. To others It can be explosive and vibrating. Paul says in Philippians 4:11 *"…I have learned in whatever state I am in to be content."* In short, he is saying, regardless of the atmosphere or the present surroundings, "be content." But some find themselves wishing time away, waiting for the next hour to pass while others are able to see time as a way to accomplish a task or set the pace for a new day, and be thankful for the time within the hours of life itself.

Most think of time as pleasing oneself and if this isn't accomplished then "time" is wasted. Verse 13 in chapter 3 of Ecclesiastes says, enjoyment from the good of your labor is a *"gift of God."* Verse 17 goes on to say, *"He has appointed a time for every matter and every work."*

Time can be a luxury for a busy person. We have all heard, "I don't have enough time." We all have the same amount of time, but some take on more activity than they have space to accomplish. Time can be the "devils' workshop" for an idle mind. We need to keep productive thoughts to keep boredom from getting us into trouble. Time can be a blessing to heal wounds. A scar might be left but "time" can heal, and an experience is left. Time can be a curse to the aged that is suffering. What is time for you? Is it time to reevaluate your life and what you do with the twenty-four hours that have been allotted to you?

Have you found time to –

- Help someone heal?
- Build someone's dreams?
- Reconstruct a life that may affect their salvation?
- Smile at someone you don't like.
- Find the good in someone by turning the bad inside out?
- To take a positive look at good and be content with the bad that has been dealt to you?

What is priority for you? Is it saving up for eternal reward or is it focused on the temporal of here and now? Remember the account of what you do now is forever held in the pages of "time" accounted. *"Do not lay up for yourselves treasures on earth, where moth and rust destroy and where thieves break in and steal; but lay up your treasures in heaven… For where your treasure is there your heart will be also."* (Matthew 6:19-21) "Consecrate me now to Thy service, Lord, by the power of grace divine, let my soul look up with a steadfast hope and my will be lost in Thine." (Second verse in the hymn, *"I am Thine*

O Lord" (written by Fanny J Crosby 1875). May this be a renewed consecration of time end in the account "paid in full" when earthly time has ended in your life, beginning now.

"The Effects of Pain"

The effects of pain scream and often display deep torturing within the walls where the pain silently steals from the victim. Pain can be physical, caused by disease and leaves its effects on the body, and daily many must succumb to that pain. Sometimes it becomes so much of one's life it almost becomes a friend, so when it is missing one would think that something must be wrong. Pain can be the effects of an accident, whether small or traumatic. The changing or the rearranging of the body within the physical structure brings pain whether slight or nearly unbearable to what David of Old tells us in Psalms that we are 'fearfully and wonderfully made." (Psalms 139:14)

There are other pains that are physical. The emotional pain is just as devastating as the body. This is usually caused by interactions with others and often it is the efforts of what one does that brings on the emotional pain in either us or those closest to us. It has come to my mind the story of King David and his son Absalom. Absalom had betrayed his father, yet when the time came for battle, David dealt with two types of pain – emotional and spiritual. He was fighting a battle that defended the "people of God," and his son was the enemy. Yet, he cautioned his soldiers to "deal gently." Absalom met a horrible death, and it was said to King David, "The Lord avenged all those who rose up against thee." (I Samuel 18:31) Still David asked, "Is Absalom safe?" The news of his inevitable death tore to the very core of his heart and King David suffered an emotional pain inflicted on a tender, loving, and forgiving heart. Many of us have suffered this pain and continue to bear the emotional scars and cannot be seen by human eyes, yet our gracious Lord sees every heartache and counts every teardrop. "…Put my tears in Thy bottle. Are they not in Thy Book?" (Psalms 56:8)

Pain from mental imbalance from the function of the brain also holds its curses. Some of us will never understand these conditions and the stigma attached to those who wear the mask that covers the pain. This brings to mind, the "demoniac" in the story that Luke tells in Chapter 8:16-39. He surely was inflicted with mental disease that was misunderstood, but thank God that He can read the mind that reaches out to Him, and understands the garble that others fail to recognize as the call for help.

I am closely acquainted with one who suffers from paranoid schizophrenia. He lived with his sister, an outcast from society at that period of time. One day without warning or prior incident, he killed his brother-in-law, whom he loved. Something went wrong within him and now he spends the rest of his life in a mental institution imprisoned with a horror that he himself inflicted on someone he loved and probably to this day is suffering the mental anguish that the demoniac also suffered.

We have touched briefly on Spiritual pain. There is a pain that teeters with commitment and non-commitment. Do we walk with Jesus, or do we stand on the sidelines in an undecided quandary? Most of this pain is based on our rejection, disapproval, or an incapability of living up to the cynical view and feel it is just too inconvenient to serve Jesus on his conditions. They persuade themselves that their actions don't count, but rather their intentions, however laid aside they may be.

Whatever your pain maybe and however justified you may feel that you are in the actions you take because of the pain you are enduring, remember dear friend, that Jesus suffered from every form of pain that you have and continue to endure. He took on that pain so He could become the High Priest for us. (Hebrews 8:1) *"Dear friends, do not be surprised at the painful trial that you are suffering, though something strange was happening to you. But rejoice that you participate in the sufferings of Christ, so that you maybe overjoyed when His glory is revealed."* (I Peter 4:12-13)

Anger is a pain in and of itself. When an injustice is done, forgiveness is part of the equation for extending forgiveness is part preparing for eternity. To forgive is not an ability to be able to do it because we care commissioned to do so for it is human to hold on to that hurt of injustice that has been done to us.

The pain and the injustice don't fade in time and just dissipate. Anger is part of the pain and the injustice that took part in the life affected. If the perpetrator does not give his or her life up to God, then they have to deal with the Almighty for it says in II Thessalonians 1:6 "God is just. He will pay back trouble to those who trouble you." (NIV) Vengeance does not belong to the created being. In the New King James Version it says, "It is a righteous thing with God to bring tribulation to those who trouble you." Hebrews 10:30 claims, "Vengeance is Mine, I will repay, says the Lord." This is called trusting in God to take care of all that has come to trouble you. This is called leaving it with the Almighty to have His day to take care of all the evil dealings in this world.

But the flip side of the coin is that God would prefer that none should perish and all would come to repentance. (See John 3:15-17). The only unforgivable sin is the sin of grieving the Holy Spirit. *"And to grieve the Holy Spirit of God by whom you are sealed for the day of redemption."* We can pray for forgiveness of someone while they are yet alive claiming the promise in I John 5:14-16. It is the power of God working in the human heart that enables that person to forgive the unforgiveable and it is the power of God that transforms the life that repents and washes the sins in the blood of Christ and puts the white robe of righteousness on the one who gives his life to Christ and is freed within to accept the gift of eternal life and walk in the light of God's love.

Those who cannot accept that the sin is not any greater than another or those who are blinded by their own sins and can only see the sins of others, are in danger of losing heaven, We all live to reap the consequences of our sins, whether it is murder, unforgiving attitude, molestation, self-righteousness, hatred, lack of self-control, malicious gossip or whatever is *not* the fruit of the Spirit. (Galatians 5:22-23) Heaven will be shared by those in the Bible that were Murderers, (Paul, Moses, David) Adulterer (David), Anger, (Moses), Drunkard, (Noah), Liars. (Abraham) when he said Sarah was his sister rather than his wife when they went to Egypt. This is just a few, for each of these names were considered righteous, holy men of God because even though they sinned terrible sins against God and man, they were forgiven much and therefore they had a greater understanding of the true meaning of forgiveness because they were given back that freedom within them that gave them the key to eternal life and freedom from the effects of their pain.

"I love You So…"

I formed you in your mother's womb,
I gave you breath out of the watery tomb.
I watched you grow in your parents' care.
I have seen your trials and the abuse you have had to bear.
I set a plan to bring you close to Me,
For your life was filled with woe and I wanted you to see
That I still had you in the palm of My hand,
And nothing escaped my Eye that I had planned.
From a child of God to a child of wrath,
So, I gave you promises that would let you know,
That amid your trials, I love you so.
I saw you weave a crooked path
From a child of God to a child of wrath,
But because you were once Mine,
I sacrificed men and life down through the ages of time,
To win you back to your rightful birth.
To give you courage and endurance with this walk on earth.
I heard your call in the middle of the night.
I saw your tears fall in despair with the strife you have had to fight,
But I placed My promises deep in your heart so you would know,
That even in the darkest hour, I love you so.
I saw you fall on your knees to pray,
As you reached out in faith for a better day.
I heard that fervent heartfelt prayer,
So, I sent ministering angels to let you know I care.
They fought the battle of darkness with a fierce clash of power,
As they were holding you in that bleakest hour.
But I commissioned them to do whatever it may take,
To save your soul for My Name's sake,

Out of the Darkness... "Freedom Within"

So, I flashed My promises in your mind to know,
That I had heard you and I love you so.
I was tempted and torn between heaven and earth
I was tortured and tried, degraded, and lost My self-worth.
I was mocked and chided, degraded, and denied.
But it was for you, my child and for those tears you have cried,
So let Me hold you close to Me,
And hold the burden that others fail to see.
For I commanded the stars to shine in the sky,
And you are My diamond for whom I died.
I hold you in the very palm of My hand so you will know,
That it was for you I died because I love you so."

(Written by Joyce A. Leonard 01-27-2001)

*"...and the earth quaked, and the rocks split
and the graves were opened..."*
(Matthew 27:51b -52a)

And the God of all flesh speaks to the hearts of His children who Love Him. If He can make the earth to quake and the rocks to split, and the graves to be opened, then He can recreate and restore that which has been stolen by the enemy. For He is the Repairer of the Breach, the Great I AM. He is a living God Who loves with the forgiving love that calls and woos the heart of man.

Does God's love stop? When we ask for God to shield us...and He does, isn't it greater to ask for that same shielding for those we love? And when we endure the pain for others, is it not that same pain that Jesus endured for us? Sometimes we have to stand on the sidelines and wait...wait for the healing process that mends the brokenness so we can enjoy the sweet sense of relief. But during the process there is a bitter burning ache that seems burdensome, but is losing one soul any easier for Him?

Does the passing of a decade make Him less interested in the lost? No. Then why do Christians feel that way when a loved one turns away, that it is okay to cease praying and quickly allow the enemy to take what our Lord died for? Does hope go away because in the marriage vow that was set as sacred before God has been trampled on and emotions die and dreams end? People think one is foolish to love one who doesn't love back. So, is our Lord foolish to love those who have cast Him away? No. Then why as His servants should we stop praying, stop caring, stop loving, if we serve Him and want to reflect His love? Do we give up because others say it should be? No, a thousand times "no." *For it is the love of God that sustains us.* "*...for He makes the sun to rise on the evil and on the good and sends rain on the just and on the unjust.*" (Matthew 5:45)

And it is the prayers of those who love God that will win back the loved one who has strayed and all heaven will rejoice if only one will repent and give glory to God.

"Forever Too Late"

Have you ever spoke a hasty word or been compelled to do a hasty act out of anger, frustration, or out of sheer desperation? And the regrets that followed the course of action are either embittered and continue or repented of and the action is rectified.

There is a law out, "three strikes and you are out," That means no turning back. You can't take the actions back or the hasty words, or the unkind accusations that may be a mixture of error and truth, but still represent a falsehood for anything that is not complete truth is a deceptive lie. Therefore, the retraction of the event is forever too late.

James 3:8 says, "*...no man can tame the tongue, it is an unruly evil full of deadly poison.*" *A soft answer turns away wrath.*" (Proverbs 15:1), but how often does one stop to consider the impact of their words once the poison has been spewed...it becomes forever too late.

Some have the ability to laugh off some unkind words and let them "roll off their back" as the saying goes, while others take every word literally to heart. The old saying, "sticks and stones may break my bones but words will never hurt me" simply isn't true. Once the hasty word that the unkind, deceitful tongue has spoken, the damage is done, and it takes much longer to heal than a broken bone.

Children especially take things literally. I remember being so angry with my youngest daughter over some incident, and the incident is long forgotten, but the words are well remembered. I said,

"If you don't stop, I am going to paste you." She fell into a fit of tears and wailed to her sister, "Mama is going to glue me to the wall." Well, that turned out to have some humor and the anger dissipated and the problem cured before it went further.

That isn't always the case, and we live to regret the words we said, and they come back and haunt us. We say things to dramatize the point, to make it effective, to make the one we are upset with to either stop their hurting action or to jar them into the reality, that unless they stop, drastic action will follow. Then sometimes we take our foul attitude out on the wrong one altogether. Some may have insight to this, but others may not – however, your words may be meant, there is an uninvited guest, a silent witness of each hasty word spoken, and each hasty action done, for Ecclesiastes 5:2 says, *"Do not be rash with your mouth, and let not your heart utter anything hastily before God."* Then Proverbs 29:20 hits you to the core with, *"Do you see a man hasty with words? There is more hope for a fool than for him."*

Someone that was dear to me wrote the following words in repentance for words he remembered saying and they haunted him later. *"I came home with the intent of going hunting, but grief weighed on my heart for I had lost my second-best friend on this earth, my dog, Toby. The thought of killing any animal was out of the question. I decided to rake and do some yard work, when I came near the corner of the driveway and noticed where the earth had been disturbed just three days ago. Toby's grave. I had a lump in my throat and remembering the words I had said, those horrible words came back to me, 'I can't wait till the dogs are gone. They are a pain in the ___. Then I said loudly, 'Toby, I always loved you.' He was a dog, my best friend and loving him now was forever too late to take back those words that will always haunt me. I didn't mean them."*

This is the consequence of those haunting words that left the repentant spirit in remorse for the act of saying something in haste. I have been guilty of hasty words and a quick action without thought to what the consequence might be. I think all of us at one time or another, but we have a God that promises to help and overthrow the enemy. (II Chronicles 20:8) our tongue, and our deeds in any battle that we face. All we have to do is call upon Him and He says, *"Before you have called, I will answer- I know exceedingly and abundantly all you ask or think."* (Isaiah 65:2, Ephesians 6:20).

But there is a time coming when there will be no turning back, and it won't be because our Lord has not been long-suffering toward us. He is coming again to receive us to Himself, and He extends the hand of mercy now, while we are yet able to receive it.

We are told to *"be angry and sin not."* We are counseled not to let *"any corrupt word to proceed out of our mouth, but what is good for necessary edification, that it may impact grace to the hearers, and not grieve the Holy Spirit of God, by Whom you were sealed for the day of redemption."* (Ephesians 4:26-30)

We need to take heed to these thoughts, for the day may come when it could be, "forever too late."

"Have You Grown Weary with Your Praying?"

Have you prayed for something for a very long time and not seen the results? Have you left the problem simmering on the back burner of your mind, thinking at some point, it will take care of itself? Do you find yourself walking away from it hoping it will work out and just go about doing your own thing? I guess it all has to do with how important the matter is to you. Is it a matter of material gain? A matter of having someone healed. And when they died, you felt your prayers were in vain? A matter of something lost and you gave up because you couldn't find it and your prayers were lost too? A matter of a job change, or a test that must be taken. Is the issue a matter of life and death?

The last question is the most important to answer because life and death involves eternal life and eternal death. Praying for the lost, and praying without ceasing, praying to search your own heart. Praying for that soul to be redeemed. How important is your family, your friends, your peers to you? Let's get really close to the heart of the matter, your spouse, your children, your father, your mother, your sister, your brother – how important are they to you? Then you need to ask, "How important is Jesus to me?" Am I willing to pray in anguish as Jesus' does for me? That's right, I said 'does.' Take the verse in Luke 22:31, and place of Simon, put your own name. "*Satan has asked to sift you like wheat*" Jesus goes on in the next verse to say, "*But I have prayed for you that your faith will not fail; and when you have returned to Me strengthen your brethren.*"

When Jesus went to the Garden of Gethsemane (Luke 22:40) He commissioned the disciples to *"pray that they enter not into temptation."* Is it a temptation to withdraw from prayer? I believe it is, for we grow weary when we don't see the results that we want. Jesus then went a little way away to be alone in prayer, In verse 44 it says, "*And being in agony, He prayed more earnestly.*" How do we agonize in prayer? – one time and no results so each time we become less in tune with the need, and we grow weary with no results.

"*During the days of Jesus' life on this earth He offered up prayers and petitions with loud cries and tears to the One Who could save Him from death, and He was heard because of His reverent submission,*" (Hebrews 3:7)

Jesus prays passionately and we should follow His example. he is the prayer partner Who is able to bring answers. "*Therefore, He is able to save completely those who come to God through Him for He lives to intercede for them.*" (Hebrews 7:25) Then we are told in James 5:16, "*.... pray for one another, that you may be healed. The fervent, effectual prayer of a righteous man avails much.*" Do you think you are righteous? The true righteous man is Jesus Christ, and His righteousness can only be applied to us by His precious blood. His prayers are the most effective and the most fervent in our behalf. He is the righteous man.

Yet, we tend to murmur and complain when our prayers take so long to receive an answer. If we believe we are praying in accordance with the will of God, do we go forth boldly or do we become faint in our prayer time forgetting from what we ourselves have just brought out of by the grace of God? Let's consider God's servant Job. We also are His servants, those of us who are truly committed to serving our

Lord, aren't we? Job's friends, and I would say they were probably church friends for they seemed to be aware of what God is able to do that Job had some unforgiven sin he had not confessed, that he needed to repent. They had all sorts of advice, and they seemed to be quite wise in their words. Have you been there? Here you are the one fervently, languishing in prayer and all those around you have the savvy and they don't really have a clue about the relationship you have with God, and how you have cried in the night in prayer and anguished over your loss and your willingness to continue in this condition until the soul for which you are praying has come to a confrontation with God on their own Damascus Road.

So, do you hear the ridicule, 'What good are your prayers?' and 'Don't you think God is trying to tell you something?' they go on with, 'Are you praying for the right thing?' They continue with 'Perhaps you are praying selfishly,' and 'Is this really God's will or it *your* will?'

They won't even let up as they continue to badger, 'You are making yourself sick, so just go about your business and stop this anguishing spirit.' For those of you who maybe going through similar circumstances, let me tell you that "God's ear is not heavy, and neither is His arm too short to save." (Isaiah 59:1) "For My thoughts not your thoughts, nor are your ways My ways," says the Lord. "For as the heavens are higher than the earth so are My ways higher than your ways, and My thoughts from your thoughts." (Isaiah 55:8-9)

Listen to the words of Job 12:2-4 *"No doubt you are the people, and wisdom will die with you! But I have understanding as well as you. I am not inferior to you. Indeed, who does not know such things as these? I am one mocked by his friends, who called on God and He answered him, the just and the blameless who is ridiculed."* Amid Job's perplexities and frustrations, it was during his soul searching that he determines in Job 13:5 **"Though He slay me I will trust Him."**

I heard an analogy of those who search out prayer partners, that they don't need to look any further than the Great Prayer Partner Himself, Jesus Christ. *"for He draws near to us when we pray, encircling us with His arm of humanity and reaching through the cosmic universe to the throne of grace and mercy with His arm of divinity praying with us, and interceding for us."* Don't grow weary dear people, with your praying for Jesus is very near listening and answering all our prayers in His time, for He has promised.

"Thy Will Be Done, Lord"

It is childlike faith that produces "the great and mighty" answers that are unknown to us. (Jeremiah 33:3) It is the prayer of faith that we can move the mighty arm of God to work in our behalf and that is what makes the promises of God so precious. It isn't God that fails with the answer; it is our unbelief that He will fulfill His word. It is like saying: I know that Jesus died for me so I can have eternal life, but I don't think I can be saved.

We know it is God's will that we are saved. Therefore, we must meet His conditions. No we probably won't be saved if we are defying His laws and doing our own thing without living for Him, but staying selfishly in our own desires without giving God the honor and glory that He deserves is blatant disrespect on our part. If we just continue a life that gives way to becoming greedy, lying and deceitful and wasting our living in pursuing our own wants without a relationship with God, our Creator, then we probably won't be saved. It is God's will that we are saved, so if we serve Him, we have nothing to fear except that we may live in denial of His promises.

When you take on the challenge of praying with intercession, it seems you are standing alone against the odds in the eyes of the world and even some in the Christian community. The counselors of the world will say, 'There is a pattern of behavioral dysfunction and so and so needs counseling. It will take years of counseling for that person to ever be right and even then it is iffy if they will ever change." Is it God's will that your child tells lies and steals? Is it God's will that your husband or wife commit adultery? Is it God's will that the molester or the rapist are never redeemed or that the murderer will never enter the Kingdom? NO!

Everyone has free will and can choose to do what is right… "Oh well!" This blasé attitude just may keep you out of the kingdom, my friend. This is where heartfelt prayer and unceasing prayer makes its entrance.

There was a man who murdered Christians – why he will never change. He brutally destroyed lives. Wait a minute! I heard he had a Damascus Road experience that he was struck by a bright light and blinded and from that moment on his life was transformed. That man was Paul who also transformed lives with inspired books in the Bible. Wow! That was a miracle then, but could it happen now? The world says, it is doubtful unless you have years of counseling.

I remember reading about another man who had committed adultery with the wife of his most faithful servant. This man was a king and could have whomever he desired, but he wanted what didn't belong to him and he actually sent his faithful servant out on the battle front where he was sure to die just so he could have this man's wife. This man is far to wicked to be saved. Once you do something like that, you just don't stop, unless you receive extensive counseling and a rebuilding of the value of life. Wait a minute! The scripture says that this man was the "apple of God's eye." (Psalms 17:8) M-m-m and the reason being, he repented and was changed. That was King David. There was a consequence he had to bear the consequences of his sins as we all bear the consequences of our wrong doing, but he had a contrite heart and even though he lived with the scars of his sinfulness, God blessed him and he became one of the greatest witnesses and songsters for God ever recorded in the books of history.

Let's consider another man who murdered an Egyptian out of anger for beating a slave. To some that may seem justifiable, but murder is murder in the eyes of God as well as in the laws of the land. He became a fugitive from justice for once he had done the wrong, he ran. This man became one of God's greatest leaders in the Bible. Moses freed many of God's people that were used as slaves, but it was done after repentance and learning how God wanted him to lead out by tending sheep in the wilderness for 40 years! That was his counseling.

I could go on with many other instances and I don't want to discredit the values of counseling for I believe a neutral position that doesn't know either side can be a good thing and a fresh slant on a given situation. I also believe that the transforming power of God that restored and gave new life to liars, murderers, thieves, and adulterers is still capable today as it was in the books of time. I believe that the Bible promises are as effective and as powerful now as they were then.

Each time we enter into another new year, many of us try to renew our vows to lose weight, finish a project, exercise more, and change our attitude to be more positive and so the list goes, but I am challenging you to renew your thinking and ask God to control your thoughts for this is His will to "work in you to do both His good will and good pleasure." (Philippians 2:13) If you are not sure if you are willing to do what He wants or is calling you to do, pray this simple prayer, "Lord, make me willing to be willing." Then put your finger on His promise in Philippians 2:13 and ask Him, believe that He has, claim the promise and just thank Him. These are the ABC's of prayer.

Make a vow to serve God daily. Call upon Him to counsel you in whatever direction He wants. If He didn't want you to prosper and be in good health (3 John verse 2) He wouldn't have said it. If He didn't want your loved one to be saved, He wouldn't have said, "He who believes in Me is not condemned:..." (John 3:18) If you are doing what God wants and you are sure of it, you can count on Him listening to you, rescuing you from your enemies, protecting you, guiding you and if you need the human counseling, He will send you there. If you read His holy word, you will be transformed and made a new person in Jesus Christ because He said so and the God I know does not lie, because he cannot lie. (Numbers 23:19) Make each day profitable in Jesus Christ as you decide to follow Him. So be it!

Let's Get It Right!

*"If I could only know the heartaches you have felt,
the longing of the things that never came,
I would not misconstrue your erring,
nor ever blame."*

CHAPTER ELEVEN

It was 1998.

The phone rang. It was my brother. "I don't know if Lisa is dead or alive?" In unbelief of what I just heard, I screamed, "What?" back into the phone. He continued, "I caught her in bed with another guy and I was so upset, I wrapped a sock around a hammer that was near by and hit her over the head with it. I thought it would knock her out and I could carry her home." Still in disbelief I was now panic stricken while trying to stay calm I replied, "And you left her there?" I could tell he was in panic mode as well and tearfully replied, "I laid her on the bed, but when I saw blood, I was scared and ran." My stomach turned and I couldn't speak. I turned to my husband and gave him the phone and went to the bedroom to my knees and began to pray in tears.

From that moment on, it was confusion, questionings, and how? What? Why? If there was anything I knew, he was a faithful husband and loved her with all of his heart. I called my pastor and informed him first and then I was going to call the authorities, but the pastor beat me to it! I didn't expect that and was confused that he would do that ahead of me when I told him I was calling them next.

In the months ahead before the court trial…my brother had run away after talking with me. His apartment was overtaken by law enforcement, guns drawn and heavy artillery ready to take him out pictured on the front page of the local paper. My brother was later found among some homeless men, drinking. His love of alcohol escalated to the bottle drinking heavily because that was what was comfortable. That was where he found acceptance.

The newspaper articles said, he broke into his ex-wife's home. It wasn't his ex-wife home at all. It was his wife and they lived together. She was having an affair and it was her brother's apartment that he went inside of and hid while his wife made love with another man. Why he hid, I don't have the answers and I am sure he doesn't either. Maybe he was going to make a surprise entrance but rather than do that, he waited. He wasn't waiting to kill her or the other guy. My brother is a movie buff and I always felt he watched too many movies and probably thought if he hit her over the head she would pass out and he could take her home, cave-man style. And they would work it out and live happily ever after. But that is not how it went.

Now, I want to be sure and let you, the reader know, that what he did I do not condone, however having been through 2 marriages that were unfaithful I can understand some of his feelings. Love can make you crazy and do things to your insides that you never thought possible.

So let me take you into a little background history. He lost his mother, our mother to a drunk driver that did not have a license. He was 5 and a half when that happened. He then was tossed here and there until our dad could get his life together after losing a wife of 34 years and left with a little boy to raise. Aunts helped here and there and that was where I came in. He was moved to live with me, a sister he didn't know because his home state was Tennessee. He was being brought up as an only child as I am 18 years older than he is. I had four children and a husband who was always belittling his family, now adding another kid to the mix brought on the worst in my husband at the time. My brother was now in the fourth grade, and when he acted out, I was always slammed with the cursings that were spewed out that he is YOUR brother as if it were a dirty word.

It was a year after he arrived, I let my dad know I couldn't be mother and dad to him and he had to take him back. He did. In that span of time, dad found a new mate and married her. Now my brother had a stepmother, and she was much to be desired in my eyes, but I knew daddy was lonely and she filled the gap.

It was six short years later. I received the news that dad had a brain tumor, and I should go see him. I took my first plane flight alone and stayed there two weeks. I felt he was going to be okay, therefore I returned home. But before I did, I promised dad that should anything happen to him, I would take my brother home with me and bring him up.

Through the teen years of raising him, he went through numerous rebellious acts and why not? He had lost 2 parents he dearly loved, and all his dreams came crashing down around him, then he had to share his life with four other kids that were his nieces and nephew but more like instant brother and sisters.

To top that, his sister that was even older than the one he was now living with did not want to take him and he felt like more of an outcast. He acted out for attention I was not able to give him while juggling a family, a job and making changes within the family unit as well as going through marital difficulties. When he was 21years of age, I asked him tearfully to leave since I had other children to worry about and his drinking was getting to be a problem.

Then he met the love of his life. Sadly, unknown to me she had filed a protection order against him in the past so that didn't look well on his record. She was taken to the hospital and treated. It was more her hands that were hurt than anything as she covered her head with her hands. Thankfully the damage was not any worse and she has been able to carry on life with another man.

I know she will wear the scars forever as we all do, and my brother still wears the scars of that act even after spending nine years in prison. He has never remarried and finds the love he misses in movies and buries himself behind the beer bottle to forget the sins of his past.

He has a natural talent when it comes to drawing and sketching. He can make the lines of a pencil come together and form the most breath-taking portraits and drawings that are worthy of a true artist. It is a God-given talent.

During his trial, I sat twenty minutes on the witness stand reviewing for the grand jury the events of his life. My prayer continues for him to find strength in Jesus to let go of those horrors of his past and rebuild his life for the Kingdom of heaven and I certainly wish that as well for the one he hurt and for healing that only comes from the Great Physician, Jesus Christ.

"A Place of Refuge"

*"Bow down Your ear to me.
Deliver me speedily; Be my rock of refuge
A fortress of defense to me."
Psalms 31:2 (NKJV)*

CHAPTER TWELVE

What comes to mind when you think of a place of refuge?

There are safe houses for battered women, shelters for the homeless, hospitals for the sick, nursing homes for those that have no where to go and need a place to go for they cannot care for themselves. Hospice, which is a place where you are comforted until death and there are churches, a place for unconditional acceptance. What about a prison? Some prisons are a safety for those who need to be contained for they are a danger to others and often times themselves.

I thought about the forts I have visited here within the State of Maine. Fort Knox being the most impressive. It has high stone walls and a dark dungeon effect as you enter within the cold stony fortress. When it was being constructed many years ago, I am sure that no electricity was available only the lighting of lanterns was used to work during the night hours yet they had to be careful for the enemy may be watching. This also brings to mind the poem by Henry Wadsworth Longfellow of the great patriotic ride of Paul Revere. That well-known poem that reflects how the lighthouses are structured to give warning, "One if by land and two if by sea," in reference to where the enemy is nearby and alerting them that danger is near. The coldness of the structure with the wintery chill coming in through the portholes where guns were stationed during times of war must have brought on much sickness.

Then Fort Western holds great significance as well being a city within a city. Augusta, which is the Capital of Maine within this fort is a settlement in the midst of the city. It is a settlement that is surrounded by what is called an open picket fence with spaces just far enough apart so no adult figure would be able to enter the open area of the settlement which is just before the closed picket fence which has no openings making the security tighter. During times of war these forts were a place of refuge.

One of the most notorious forts in San Francisco Bay, which held famous inmates such as Al Capone, and has a history of being the inescapable place for prisoners. Three men, Frank Morris and the Anglin Brothers escaped which to this day, they have never been found. It was thought they might have made it to Angel Island 2.5 miles away, but highly unlikely with the cold waters, wind and current. The Island itself is 1.5 miles from the shores of San Francisco. Yet, no bodies have ever been recovered nor has any evidence that they made it to the mainland, which if they had, they would have changed their identity. Alcatraz was also a place for the "Indians of all Tribes" to come together in 1969, and they were honored here for 19 years. This extensive fort that became a military incarceration place during times of war, a maximum security for inmates that had committed treason, a federal penitentiary founded first by Spanish explorer, Juan Manuel de Ayala in 1775. It was sold to the US government in1854 and became the first lighthouse. These are considered a place of safety reaching out to those in trouble and in need of refuge. Now this Island is a National Park, and this interesting history is given in the tours of those who visit. (Information gathered from Wikipedia and Britannica)

The Hebrew word for 'refuge" is quelat which means to contact, to draw, to take in, to relieve. There were Cities of Refuge during Bible times that were literally places of holiness set apart for sacred use, much different than the places of refuge we see today. These cities were needed because of ridicule, rejection, threat or just because you claimed to be a Christian. In Numbers Chapter 35 gives detailed information on these cities of refuge. It seems it was the duty of the Sanhedrin, which were the church leaders was to provide a roadway of safety to congregation to judge in mercy and restore. To judge means "causing release." In Deuteronomy Chapter 19 it also instructs for three specific cities and their responsibility to those under the jurisdiction.

Numbers 35:12-15 read (NKJV)

"They shall be cities of refuge for you from the avenger, that the manslayer may not die until he stands before the congregation in judgment.

And the cities which you give, you shall have six cities of refuge.

You shall appoint these cities on this side of Jordan, and three cities you shall appoint in the land of Canaan, which will be cities of refuge.

The six cities shall be for refuge for the Children of Israel, for the stranger, and for the sojourner among them, that anyone who kills a person accidentally may flee there."

The King James Version says, *'kills them unaware."*

There was a report on the news that in 2019 that a correctional officer was on his way home from a double shift and fell asleep at the wheel crashing into another vehicle and killing the 9-year-old girl in the car with her daddy. He was now standing trial in 2022. I have not at this writing seen the outcome of that trial, but at the time of reading the account, I felt this man needed a place of refuge. I prayed for him. The point can be made that whatever we do and whatever happens there are consequences to our choices. He didn't feel tired, so he drove and fell asleep. I thought back to the times I drove school bus and pulled an all nighter taking the senior graduating class to a university to party all night in an nonalcoholic environment and brought them back to the school in the wee morning hours then went on to do the day trips without having any sleep. Now I could have slept in the bus (uncomfortably) and probably not a good sleep, but I chose to be with the kids and their activities. I did not have the tragic accident he did. I am sure it will or has been brought out that he should have been more conscientious of his lack of sleep and found another way home. We all face unforeseen circumstances that we never thought would happen to us. He has to live with the fact that his choice caused the death of a little girl accidently, unaware of it happening and to me that is a sentence within itself.

If you are serving God as a Christian, you are to provide a place of refuge for the suffering, a place of shelter to those who are threatened by obstacles that are not of their own choosing, a place of comfort. We do not all have the physical means to provide to the sojourner, the one who is homeless and no where to go. The shelters are full. The nursing homes are overcrowded, and the price is far more than one has. You become an award of the State and whatever you have they take. The place of refuge is a sanctuary of safety. Some go out and commit a crime just to go to jail because it is a place of safety. a place to keep warm and get a meal.

Let's go back to the six Cities of Refuge. They were consistently distanced to accommodate the 12 tribes. They were a sanctuary for the fugitive. It was the business of the leaders of the church to maintain the roadway and keep them in good condition, bridges in repair and cleared of any debris making the roadway assessable for the fugitive. Judges and elders were stationed at the city gates to transact all legal business to the vagabond that traveled there. This is a good illustration of what the Christian life is supposed to consist of.

Jesus is the "place of refuge" where the sinner can flee.

Three of the cities were located on the west side of the Jordan River and three were east of it. Those on the west were Kadesh, in the land of Naphtali, a place to be *holy*. Shechem in the western part of Manasseh's inheritance, a *place of readiness to bear burdens*, and Hebron in the land of Judah, a place of *fellowship*. Those on the east side of Golan in the land of Bashan meaning *their captivity, their rejoicing*. Ramoth-Gilead was a place called for the *exalted* and Bezer, in the land of Rueben a *fortress*. These all represent the forts and the places of refuge of today but even more they represent Christ. He is the refuge for the guilty sinner. The roadways are open with signposts along the way making access to the city of refuge easier. *Fellowship, carrying one another's burdens* illustrates that Jesus is our great *Burden Bearer*. Taking time to be *holy* and we are told we are to be holy even as He is holy. (see Leviticus 11:44, I Peter 1:16) God provides a fortress to surround His children from the enemy, and all we have to do is call upon His name. He is to be *exalted* and reverences for He is God and worthy to be praised. Jesus said:

> "All that the Father gives Me will come to Me, and the one who comes to Me, I will in no way cast out."
> (John 6:37) NKJV

The church is to be the best place of refuge. It should emulate the love of God as those who come in the doors who are broken and feel the look of disdain from those around them who judge them with the unrighteous heart. This is to be a haven of safety from the world of chaos and troubles. A place where whatever happens we can come and feel that someone understands. In saying this, it isn't always the way. Sadly this is often a reason or an excuse to leave church or the unrighteous one who came in judges those that are within, forgetting they are human, and humans fail, but Jesus never fails.

Do you remember playing hide and seek as a child? You hurried to find a safe place, a secret place to hide where you couldn't be found. A place that was so secure that the pursuer could walk right past you and not even know that you were there. Do you remember feeling your excitement about your place of safety, knowing you found a "safe place." As soon as the seeker had past and was out of sight to know where you had been hiding, because you certainly wouldn't want them to know where your safe place was in case of another time around, you then quickly run and tag your goal.

Every day our pursuer is Satan, and the Bible tells us that in I Peter 5:8 *"...your adversary, the devil walks around like a roaring lion, seeking who he can devour,* Within the human element there is a desire to be known and know others with the ability to say how you feel and find acceptance and find agape love. The church should specialize in broken hearts. I John 3:16-18 says (NKJV) *"By this we know love, because He laid down His life for us. And we ought to lay down our lives for the brethren. But whosoever has this world's goods, and sees his brother in need, and shuts up his heart from him, how does the love of God abide in Him? My little children, let us not love in word*

Out of the Darkness... "Freedom Within"

or in tongue, but in deed and in truth." You know the old says rings true here, "Actions speak louder than words."

FORT KNOX – BUCKSPORT, ME

FORT WESTERN – AUGUSTA, ME

Joyce A. Leonard

As we look for a place of safety, a secret place,
hidden from the molesting eye.
A place where peace and joy entwine along the eastern sky.
A place where death's door is beaten down,
Where healing grace does abound.
As I walk along the narrow path in quiet solitude,
I can still hear the whispers of ridicule that brood.
While in the distance, bombs of chaos are tossed about,
Ravaging fear and causing doubt.
O place of refuge – a great need,
To be a place where no one can overtake with greed,
For the meager supplies that have been cast aside,
From those who have prayerfully cried.
The time is at hand, my friend.
Listen carefully to the lies that blend,
Creating a space that questions within the mind
Voicing unbelief and displaying critical find.
Take refuge in the city of hope and listen to Jesus Holy Word.
Gird up your loins with truth and the promises heard.
Don't let Satan steal eternity and win the fight.
Jesus died for you to be able to make the choice that is right.
Secure us O God in the battle of injustice fought.
Keep us safely under what the Almighty has wrought,
Reaching ahead for the banner of truth and love,
While piercing the darkness with redemption of our God above.

By Joyce A. Leonard 12-29-2022

Freedom Promised

"Risky Business"

*"And this is the promise
that He has promised us Eternal life."
I John 2:25*

CHAPTER THIRTEEN

It had been decided that Jenny and Penny were going to meet on the road between their two homes after everyone had gone to bed. They lived about a quarter of a mile apart and it was giving them excitement that drenched their minds as they anticipated their caper. "Don't forget," Penny reminded Jenny. "I don't want to risk getting caught if you aren't going to show up!" Jenny answered her friend with a light-hearted "Don't worry."

It wasn't a school night and the girls had mischief in mind. Lights were out and Jenny put her plan into action. She slipped her pajamas on over her clothes and began her trek down over the stairs that went past her parents bedroom door to the winding staircase that finally reached the first floor of their big ole' farmhouse. At each creak in the wooden boards of the staircase, she stopped and waited with her heart pounding so loud, she was almost sure her parents could hear it from their bedroom and would awaken. When she was sure no one heard that one, she moved on to the next until she had completed her decent and was safely on the front porch. She carefully slipped off her pajamas and tucked them securely under the pillow that rested on the cot that occupied the screened in front porch. Hurriedly she raced down over the lawn onto the street and breathlessly half trotted toward Penny's house. She was on her way to freedom. It might have been risky but the excitement that raced through her veins outweighed any thought of failure.

The plan had been carefully laid that they were going to hitch hike to the nearest town where the "action" was and to be part of it for a couple hours, then to return home the way they had left. It was unusually dark out and no streetlights added to the inky blackness. The little town they lived in was so small many people didn't realize they had passed through it before they were out of it! There was no excitement here. They swam in the lake, and played football with the neighborhood boys, and ice skated out back of the library at the fire station. That was the extent of any excitement.

The grave yard was settled between their two homes, and it was kind of a scary place to go by. As Jenny approached the cemetery, fear tightened in her heart as she held her breath, she went on a dead run until she was safely on the other side of the perimeter of the graveyard.

Reaching Penny's house, it seemed like Penny was not anywhere to be found. Thoughts manifested that Penny had fallen back to sleep. "Penny, Penny" Jenny called out in a hoarse whisper as loud as she dared. No answer. Jenny picked up a stone and shot it up at Penny's bedroom window, hoping it would just tap the window pane enough to wake her up. SMASH! Glass was tinkling as it landed on the inside on the floor while some of it fell outside on the roof of the porch that was just under Penny's bedroom window. Jenny darted behind the big Maple tree in the front yard that stood by the roadside. "Penelope what are you doing?" Penny's mom was some mad as she screamed out into the darkness from the porch inner doorway. There was no response and Jenny sure wasn't going to say anything. Her mother screamed again. "Penelope, get in here! she demanded.

To Jenny's amazement, Penny answered as she was coming down the road from the direction that Jenny had just come from. "I'm coming. I'm coming." Penny's tone sounded disgusted. "What on earth are you doing out at this time of night?" Penny's mother was expecting some answers and they better be good. Penny retorted quite honestly, "I was going to meet Jenny." Her mother snapped back at her, "Jenny is home on bed where you should be." Jenny never moved a muscle from her spot by the Maple tree. She closed her eyes when a car passed with its headlights glaring on her. She was sure Penny would notice her as she passed her making her way back into the house, but there was never any acknowledgment that she had been seen.

She could hear Penny's mom giving her the dickens as she moved from her spot of safety and ran all the way back home without stopping. Yes, it was risky business doing something you know is wrong and hoping you won't get caught. Penny and Jenny were grounded from seeing each other for a good long time after that little plan went awry. I am sure as the girls look back on it later in life that, it wasn't worth the trouble.

"Risky Business"

Playing dangerous games with a silly dare
Isn't worth the consequences that the game would bear.
Fun lasts for such a short time,
And the punishment is hardly worth the crime.
The act can fade eventually but the memory doesn't forget,
When risky business is a teenager's outlet.
But when you risk heaven and what is held in store,
The stakes are higher and worth so much more.
Sin can start with just a thought
Being carried out is the risk that is wrought.
For the thought can become an act,
And the act can become a fact.
Then it is too late to turn back after what is done,
And undo the damage of what was thought fun.
So, it seems it is better not to be too frisky,
For the business of life can be quite risky.

By Joyce A. Leonard (9/03/2000)

"Straight Talk" by Michael Braiser former inmate at Maine State Prison

"My testimony, though sad, is not uncommon today where violence, drugs and sex seem to have become more popular with every passing year. However, what is uncommon (though it seems to be happening more than ever), and this is what my messed-up life was.

Let me tell you the story of how it went from being out of control and addicted to violence, drugs and sex – to coming to know the Lord and finding peace and joy beyond my capacity to understand.

I grew up in a very violent home from the age of 7 years old until age eleven. I was used as a punching bag for my stepdad who was a 5th degree black belt. I lived this childhood nightmare for 4 years. My family was torn apart and turned against each other. It wasn't bad enough that we had a monster for a dad beating us, my mom also beat me, and as children we beat on each other. Worse than the beatings was the fear that never left me during those 4 years. The fear drove me crazy and to numb that fear I turned to drugs and alcohol.

By the time I was 12, I was an alcoholic and well on my way to being addicted to marijuana. I was known as a thief and a troublemaker. I didn't have many friends because I picked fights with everybody. I had four years of anger pent up inside and I wanted to take it out on this world. When I was eleven years old I tried to kill my family and my step father by burning down the apartment we lived in. I couldn't stand seeing my family suffer. I just couldn't stand the fear of abuse any longer. Nobody was killed or died from that fire, (Thank you, God), but I was removed from my family and put in foster custody. This would start the long revolving door syndrome. I was placed in one institution after another, one foster home after another. I never stayed in one place long, because I was extremely wicked, always lashing out at my peers, and the adults.

Finally the courts just said, 'enough is enough.' It didn't seem like any amount of love or treatment was ever going to change me, so I was shipped off to the Maine Youth Center and basically forgotten about. I spent 2 1/2 years at the M.Y.C. that seemed uselessly unproductive. When I got out, I turned to drugs, crime and bad relationships. I became like my stepfather, abusive and no care of who I hurt. I went through girlfriends, one a month or more. One by one these women left because I was abusive to them.

I couldn't hold a job or a girlfriend, so, I did what I knew best. I stole, fought, and sold drugs. Whatever it took to make sure I could supply my own habit. By the time I was 20 years old, I was out of control and addicted to crack cocaine. I had become a nobody and life had no happiness for me. I had no reason to live nor any desire. I had given up on family, friends, and myself. In March of 1996, I was arrested for a series of armed robberies in the Waterville, ME area as well as for six days I was on an alcohol and drug binge. I did whatever drug I could get my hands on. In those six days I was trying to kill myself in a drug overdose. I didn't care if I got caught for the robberies I was committing. Nothing in my life mattered.

I was sentenced on July 10, 1996, to 15 years in prison. All but eight were suspended. I went to Windham, Maine Correctional where I continued to drink, steal, do drugs and fight. After two years. I tried to escape and ended up in Super Max in Warren, Maine where I spent 17 months and rediscovered God.

If those of you reading this story today find yourself relating to any part of this then I urge you to read closely. If you seek the same peace and joy that I have today, then I will share with you a free gift that is yours for the taking if you only ask.

I won't tell you that it is easy being a Christian especially in prison, but I will tell you this. If you give your life to Christ, completely to Him, and you trust Him with your everyday life, God will take care of you and bless you richly. Since coming to the Lord, I have been blessed many times over, and one of the biggest blessings is being reunited with my own father whom I had never known. My friends, God isn't a myth. He is real and alive and He is willing to bless you, if you only come to Him and *ask* for Him to come into your heart.

(Taken from the newsletter "Youth at Risk Ministry" called "Freedom Promised," a branch of "Freedom Within" by Joyce A. Leonard & Pauline Nota. Volume 1, Issue 2. Michael Braiser is the writer of the Chapter Five – on "Rage.")

"Behind These Bars" by *Robert Salo* a former inmate of Maine State Prison– writer of *"Behind These Walls"* now deceased)

"Imagine for a moment you are home; you're doing your homework and the boom box is playing excessively loud. (**Note** – not many boom boxes now, the computer and cell phones have taken the arena). You are eating your favorite (hot pockets and pizza rolls), your cat is curled up on the bed next to you and the dog is laying on the rug on the floor. Life can't get any better than this. Then there is a loud crash that resounds from wall to wall, as you jump with a start turning evasively, you suddenly realize it was all a day dream, you are not at home anymore. The loud crash was the cell door slamming shut as they prepare to count assuring society that you are still behind bars, right where you are supposed to be.

In an instant, life as you know it can change. A decision to do something can have catastrophic repercussions, one that can land you behind bars or plant you six feet under. If you are reading this column, you won't find any candy coating, for I believe you have already been told the party line. I will try to head to a non-profane manner in which to explain what I have to say, but that will be about it for gentleness.

Since this is geared for the juvenile age group, I figured you had not graduated to the adult prison system. The operative word is 'yet.' I missed out at the juvenile detention trip, and also the smaller, lesser facilities known as correctional centers and jumped headfirst into Maximum Security Prison. Like the Monopoly game, I did not pass 'GO' nor did I collect $200. Instead I collected 50 years of detention quite a few more than I ever planned to do.

I was one of those guys that never flinched at loud noises. You could threaten my life and I wouldn't be overly concerned. I didn't fear anything. I just knew I was the 'baddest' mother anywhere. When they arrested me and threw me in jail, I wasn't scared. I could depend on my father to get me out of anything. He always had and why should this time be any different? I remember my first night inside, thinking this was going to be a breeze. What's difficult about this? The first night dragged into the next day, and then the next night and so forth. Tonight, marks the 8,033 nights behind bars. This has been no walk in the park, and definitely no breeze, and while my Heavenly Father can do anything, I found out my earthly father cannot.

I made it to my 23rd year of life, before it all came crashing down on top of me. Life now was never going to be the same. I was young and a young man in prison, the same as young women in prison, they have to make a name for themselves pretty quick or else they become prey to the diverse factions that roam around behind these walls. You can be the ugliest individual in the world, but you are the newest piece of meat on the compound, and someone just has to have a taste of it. You can run to protective custody, that is if you can get there, or you can submit starting an unending chain of assaults until your release, being passed from one pimp to another, or you can stand your ground and fight back, knowing that fighting results in disciplinary infraction, and even then the assaults may not end there. I chose to fight, and figure when the individuals awoke in the infirmary they decided on another victim because that was my first and last encounter.

I'm going to jump ahead in our little history lesson here and tell you after my short comings and disastrous decisions, I finally met a man named, 'Jesus.' Even though I had heard His name before, I felt it was time to change my life. John 3:16 says, 'For God so loved the world that He gave His only begotten Son, that whosoever believed in Him should not perish but have everlasting life.'"(John 3:16)

(Note – Even though this was focused to reach Youth, this is a ministry to reach at whatever level you are in to find the Man, Jesus so that your life will be changed and if you have not experienced these things, that you will not have to if you are willing to walk after right living choosing life in Christ.)

Freedom Promised Part II

"The Price of Mischief"

*"A heart that devises wicked plans,
and feet that are swift to running to mischief."*
Proverbs 6:18

CHAPTER FOURTEEN

Did you have intercourse?

Jenny sat staring this white-haired, square jawed, tall thin man with a peaked nose that jutted out over his face as his most prominent feature. He was the town constable. He was demanding an answer to the details of her activities that day. "What is he asking, Jenny thought to herself as she wildly reviewed in her mind her own actions in silent thought. She continued to reason in her mind, 'it must be pretty bad because he is angry.' She continued to review within herself as she considered his question.

Jenny was thirteen and in the eighth grade. She had just been caught walking the railroad tracks home instead of being on the bus, and it was her mother who caught her. That morning which seemed forever ago now, she had taken the bus to school, but when she got off the bus in front of the Junior High school entrance, she turned left and kept walking toward the outskirts of town. It was almost officially summer, and it just seemed too nice to sit in a stuffy classroom. She had never skipped school before, but there is a "first time for everything," she remembered hearing her mother say that. and it just seemed like the thing to do.

It wasn't long before she met some classmates on their way to school. Three of her male classmates who lived in town close enough to walk. Hey, Jenny, where are you going, they questioned. "I am skipping school today," she curtly answered with a sparkle of mischief in her eye adding "do you wanna come along?" Pete the leader of the three answered, "No foolin'? with a grin stretching across his face as he stopped to consider the thought. "So, what would we do, he questioned further?"

"Go swimmin'," Jenny quickly retorted with a mater-of-fact attitude. After all what else would you do on such a beautiful day. Bobby and Mike decided they better not but Pete took her up on her invitation and they were off for the nearest covered bridge that was an antiquated structure in town that stretched over the river.

Jenny was unaware that her French teacher had been watching out the window and watched her leave the school grounds, then called Jenny's mother. Swimming was great. Unashamed Jenny took off her pants and swam in her underwear and blouse, while Pete took off his shirt and left his trousers on. They chased each other in their contest of agility with maneuvering in the water. After their exhausting swim, they divided what they had in their lunch sacks then laid in the tall grass in the field surrounding the riverbed to dry off.

It just seemed natural that when Pete reached over and kissed her on the lips that she returned his advance. At first it seemed kind of funny. It wasn't like the first kiss that she got in the first grade from Donny or when Curtis kissed her under the streetlight in the fifth grade. Pete's teeth were in the way and jammed up against her top lip and pinched it, but she didn't want to hurt his feelings, so she didn't say anything. He reached over to fondle her breast that had just begun to develop. She allowed it for a few minutes then pushed his hand away as she was starting to feel queasy in her stomach and a little nervous. She realized what time it was and jumped-up exclaiming, "Wow, I have a long walk ahead, so I better get going." Jenny dressed quickly and ran across the field calling back to Pete, "See you in school tomorrow."

She couldn't remember if he answered, she was in too much of a hurry. She picked up the momentum of skipping the ties on the track that were too close together and hopped the gap of those that were spaced further apart to make up for lost time. Jenny was deep in her thoughts about her day with Pete and looked up and could see a figure coming her direction. It looked like it was Mama. And what was she swinging? It was a willow switch. Jenny thought to herself out loud, "Well might as well face the music" as she came closer to her mother. She felt the sting of the willow switch across the back of her legs all the rest of the way home and mother's scathing rebuke of her disobedience.

As those thoughts fleeted through her mind, she realized now sitting in this 1958, roomy Chevy wagon being interrogated that she better give an answer. Hesitantly, "no-o-o:" Jenny answered. He scowled at her while closely scrutinizing her reply and asked, "Do you know what I am asking you?" Indignant that he would question her knowledge, for Jenny didn't like to think she was stupid, so she quickly answered "Yes." So, he quizzed again in demanding tones, "So did you?" She retorted back in disgusted tone, "No" while thinking maybe she had and didn't know it, after all Pete did touch her breasts. "Are you willing to be checked," he pressed? She wondered what they were going to check but agreed to his question. With that he drove her to her home while mother was waiting in the driveway furiously pacing. He took mother aside in the house for a few minutes then returned releasing her to Mama.

Jenny's aunt was visiting from out of state, and she took Jenny in another room and asked her, "Did that boy do anything bad to you?" Her blue eyes were gently searching Jenny's face. Jenny confessed all that happened that day to her beloved aunt. She felt free to tell her the whole story of the events for there was no judgment or condemnation, just loving concern.

After Jenny told the story to her aunt, then Aunt Ruth took the story to mother and the Constable. He left glowering at Jenny and mother sent her to her room with the warning that followed that her father would deal with her later. Caught in the act of having fun and paying the price for mischief isn't always worth the end result.

"The Price of Mischief"

A day of fun
In the warming sun.
With a cup of mischief to be drank,
While teasing and laughing at the riverbank.
What is the price of skipping school,
Showing off and being cool,
Tasting the sweetness of youth's appetite,
Touched with innocence forbidden bite!
Mischief has ways of carrying a price tag,
While learning holds a warning flag,
That obeying the rules never gets caught
Swimming in the river or not!
Youth lives for the moments cost
Testing the water where others have lost.
Thinking their fate won't be the same,
After all isn't it just pleasure's game?
"To do mischief is like the sport to fool,"
Even for a moment it seems like it is cool.
The price tag is sometimes hidden inside.
When the heart speaks as your guide
Don't toss the thoughts of doing right
"As out of mind and out of sight"
For the price may be more than you want to pay,
And then it will be too late to have a say.
By Joyce A. Leonard 03/13/2001

*"To do evil is like sport to a fool,
But a man of understanding has wisdom."
Proverbs 10:23 {NKJV}*

"Behind These Bars" by Robert Salo

"Do not be yoked together with unbelievers, for what does righteousness and wickedness have in common? Or what fellowship can light have with darkness? What harmony is there between Christ and Belial? What does a believer have in common with an unbeliever? What agreement is there between the temple of God and idols? For we are the temple of the living God. As God has said "I will live with them, and I will be their God and they will be My people." II Corinthians 6:14-16

My last letter to you was ended with scripture, so now I will begin with the scripture. I try not to tell anyone what they should do because that is what everyone else does. I hope to be able to give you an alternate direction from which you may or may not achieve a victory over some of the foul ups in your life. God knows that I have made my share of mistakes so who am I to tell anyone what they should do. I have a ruder, something to give me direction in my life, and that is the Word of God, the Bible.

I guess you could say that I was a bad apple from day one. I was arrested on June 28, 1978, in Stuben County, Indiana. I was a fugitive from justice and I was held until the State of Maine State Police came to get me. I was transported back to Maine where I was arraigned on the charge of murder. I remained in the custody of Knox County Jail in Rockland, Maine to await trial. When I messed up, I messed up big time. I was of the attitude that I was probably never going to get out, then I could do anything I wanted, and there was nothing else the authorities could do that would be any worse. So, on my third day of incarceration Knox County Jail, I attempted to escape. I did pretty good too! I took out the first officer on the scene, and his back up didn't do any better. Then the third officer wasn't much help either. Now granted, I was still inside the building, but I noticed the door was slightly ajar so, off I went!

I hit the door like a freight train and hit another officer and sent him reeling. Some idiot left the cruiser running in the parking lot and I made a bee line for it. I made it into the front seat and had just started to put it in reverse when out of nowhere came a smooth barrel of a 12 gauge shot gun!

He was yelling about choices, about life and death situation and he instructed me to put my hands behind my head and interlock my fingers or die. Not much of a choice and this officer didn't look like he was strung too tight, so I opted for LIFE instead of DEATH. Well, you can probably guess the rest. They dragged me back inside and commenced to whoop on me. Out of all the angry faces there, was one that shone through like no others, and it was the head Sheriff. He was dragging officers off from me and putting me into a cell. They ruptured my blood vessels in my wrist, with the tightest handcuffs I have ever felt.

I was transported to the State Prison in Thomaston, Maine for safe keeping, for they were unsure of the other officer's intentions toward me. I remember Captain Kiskila's first words to me, 'Welcome to the Big House. I am the boss here under the Warden and if you try anything like you did at my prison, you will have to answer to me!' Well, to make a long story short, never tell someone who has a problem with authority that they can't do something because they always do.

These episodes of my life are true and documented. But like the choices I faced concerning LIFE and DEATH in the county jail, you have the opportunity to face them in your life, except you can face them early enough in life (if you are reading this account and have never had trouble with authority) to spare you hell on earth of prison life, and you can opt for LIFE, eternal life with Jesus Christ." (John 3:16)

The Power of a Badge

CHAPTER FIFTEEN

"The Lord guards the lives of His faithful ones."
Psalms 97:10 (NIV)

I couldn't find what I was looking for in the grocery store, so I scanned around to find someone that was wearing an emblem of identity to help me with what I was looking for. The service of these types of individuals is usually courteous, helpful, and pleasant. Then there are those who wear a badge identifying themselves as Customer Service and they too provide that helpful information and usually are informative and ready to serve you with a smile. Of course, there is always one who defies that origin. There are other persons that wear a badge or an emblem of identity which entails the Boy Scout, the Girl Scout and their service is one of honor to be helpful and learn to be a credit to the community in which they grow up in. There are those who are at seminars that wear a name tag that serves to show they are the one to seek out for assistance. These emblems and badges are signs that show rank and authority that are actually a form of service. The most credible badge is the badge worn by military service men and women, hospital workers, and the officers of the law…policemen. Most of these individuals are pledged to be helpful and considerate for they serve the people. They are in the order of service.

    I have lived in my town for over 50 years and have seen a number of Chief of Police come and go. One Police Chief sent me a letter asking me to keep my dog out of the road because the traffic had to go around him while he was laying in the road. I wish I had kept that letter. It sounds humorous now. I was quite impressed and called and told him I would make sure he didn't go out in the road as his spot to lay down. Back then dog licenses were not required, and everyone was respectful of those in the community especially if they served to help the community which I did as a First Responder and graduating to EMT, and a school bus driver. I knew the town officials and then the kids in town that became police officers. My car broke down and was on the side of the road and I received a call that the officer was going to have it towed. I knew him as a kid and said, "…the registration is in the glove compartment and I will take care of it. You leave it alone. I know you and you know me so there is no need to cause me any more grief than what I am going through right now." And he did. It was taken care of at the end of the day.

But the town has grown up and with each new Chief, there was new authority. I was speeding with a school bus with one student on my bus which is still considered a full bus. The Chief came and took the ticket I received since being a rookie school bus driver, it would have probably cost my job. This Chief realized I had been reprimanded and the ticket was blotted out as if it had never existed.

Now in my latter years having seen the attitude of so many officers, it has seemed that many become prideful when they wear a badge. Pride that doesn't go the extra mile to be helpful but a pride that causes those in a small town to become angry at the business of officers who take their badge of power above what they should. After all they are to serve the community, which should not tear it apart. My mother often quoted, "You can get more flies with honey than with vinegar." I have heard some say who wants to catch flies, but the meaning escapes them. This is an analogy that has been used throughout generations to show that kindness is more attractive and a better way to obtain the end result of what you may want.

Since I have ministered within the prison community and served as on advocate for many in the five years while I was in Prison Ministry, I never thought the day would come that my son would also be in that same situation. At this writing, I will not entertain all that happened to him during his 2 years in Fort Dix Federal Prison, but I will tell you about a few officers that that did not hold their badge with a reverence of their duty toward those they guard.

During my son's stay he went in with diabetes as well as other health issues. He carried his medications with him as he self-surrendered after his trial and had been given opportunity to get his things in order before being incarcerated. He gave his medications to the officer who inducted him into prison, with his prescribed meds from his doctor. and they promptly disposed of them. They only gave out what they decided what was best without making the right judgment calls. In the process of his health deteriorating, he ended up on the bathroom floor with internal bleeding. The Lieutenant that was on duty that night, yanked him by the arm, displacing his shoulder with the words that are forever engraved on my son' ears, "You are going to Paradise tonight and you are going alone." From that point he ended up in the hospital. At the federal junction they have a closed-circuit email for inmates to keep in touch with family. I had not heard from my son so made numerous phone calls to many with no response. It was not until a couple weeks later, I threatened the Warden's office that if I did not receive a call back I would be on his doorstep with the media within 24 hours. I had every intention of making good on this threat for it was more of a promise. I received the phone call saying they were "compelled to return my call." Well, of course they were. They were fearful of a lawsuit. They proceeded to inform me that they "never call an inmates family unless the inmate is on life support or dead." My son was in the hospital with internal bleeding. It was another inmate that found him and called the guard who did nothing because she was drunk! This inmate called other inmates and they prayed over my son. I thank God for those men.

    Without going into detail of the incredible situations he endured and the miles he walked just in the outside yard to get exercise, for it was the God of heaven that had His eye on my son and carried him through the issues he went through. You see if it had been a state issue, by giving up a name of someone you can be released for the bigger "fish in the pond." But my son refused to give out that information for the situation he found himself in was not one that was a normal circumstance and he used to always say, "Don't do the crime if you can't do the time." He lived by that. He was doing his time and would not involve another person as often officers try to harass you in to doing and make all kinds of promises they cannot keep.

As his family we visited once a month making the long trek from Maine to New Jersey and staying the weekend in a motel that accommodated us greatly with four children. During those times of visitation, my granddaughter was wearing a pair of farmer jeans that had metal buckles on them. Previously the guard that I had observed that was on duty that particular day, I had misjudged. He was tattooed to the hilt, spiked hair, looking like Mr. Tough Guy, which left a bad impression with me. But while having my granddaughter go through the metal detector, the buzzer kept going off. He made the declaration to his colleagues, "She is only four, I am letting her through and if anyone has a problem they can see me." My thoughts of him instantly changed. Compassion was in his veins.

There were others that didn't quite meet my criteria with their attitudes. But they are the ones in control. I met the Chaplain and his words directly to me in a conversation I was having with him was, "My duty is to government first and God second." I lost all respect for this man who wore the badge of obedience to the Law of God. His apparent job rights were prideful in the respect of self-serving.

I recognize that there are now harder times in the police force and the different aspects of the departments represented. These men often put their lives on the line for the service of a community and the rights of protecting others. I applaud them and they deserve the praise of the country for which they serve as people they try to work with and for. Many who go out on the limb to cover those who are in depression, homeless, abused and children. Let's not forget the children they protect. But the ones who rise in the arena of dictatorship, those who forget basic human rights or label different ones as one size fits all – they should let go of the almighty badge and step down and away from their post and become part of the society that they once served.

As a former EMT I have worked with police officers that protected me from gruesome scenes and helped me through the times of sheer terror in situations. For those men I am grateful and I am glad they were in my corner at that time. I appreciate their compassion, their consideration and the times of great service.

I have seen the reactions of those who are visiting inmates and their indifference toward the visitor. Then there are those who made a difference with their kindness and their thoughtfulness and to those I say Kudo's to you for you will "catch more flies with the honey" displayed than "with the vinegar" of sourness that depicts a bad attitude and involves it in others used as a leverage of coercion.

"The Lord is righteous, He loves justice;
Upright men will see His face."
Psalms 11:7 (NIV)

Hope During a Time of Hopelessness

CHAPTER SIXTEEN

*"'For I know the plans I have for you,' declares the Lord,
'Plans to prosper you and not to harm you,
plans to give you a hope and a future.'"
(Jeremiah 29:11) NIV*

"We better get to bed early; we need to be up at 2:00 am to head for Ft. Dix." This was a family affair and instructions were being rattled off to everyone that might be listening. David was filled with instructions for his wife, Susan to make sure this and that was done as well as how it was to be done without fail. It seemed like it was a race, and why did we wait for so long to do it? But we hadn't really, because deep down we were waiting for the grand finale…a miracle. Now the deadline was here. It felt like the shadow of death sentence waiting for the axe to drop. No one disappointed us. Susan's sister arrived with her new car for us to take to Ft. Dix for the 8-hour trip. The neighbors came from across the road, and everyone was grasping for David and holding him in their arms and giving a farewell hug. No one expressed thoughts beyond the moment. There were no tears, just smiles and light chatter.

Just before bedtime, Susan raced to Rite Aide Pharmacy for his prescriptions that had been refilled. While she was gone, I got the twins ready for bed. Noah and Jaidyn had been dropped off by their mom earlier and David took his children and caressed them to his heart one more time. No one had to point a finger and say, "if only you had done this or that, this day wouldn't be happening." How many times this had rerun through his mind, only Jesus knows. And he would tell you, 'The silver lining is' his heart is with Jesus now and he has a new lease on life with Jesus.' What greater joy can a Christian mother ask for?

I went to bed, tired and needing rest when the phone rang. Then I heard David talking to our cousin Jim, a strong advocate in Prison Ministry and he called to give David hope with a story, *"Jim had been working with a man who had made a new commitment to Christ, and he was sent to prison. In a very violent prison in TN. One day a fellow inmate took this man aside and asked, 'Who is the big guy who is always with you?' The man knew there was no one with him but finally concluded God had His guardian angel visible to other inmates and no one dared to attempt any harm to him."*

God is our rearguard. He forgives when no one wants to or refuses. God is love and whatever the reason David had to go through the fire and walk in the water. But the promise is he will not be burned, and he will not be overtaken by the overflow. God bless our cousin Jim for that phone call and the words that touched my son's heart. Then a door slammed outside. Now who is here, I thought, getting pretty upset, we needed to get some sleep. It was the couple who were renting David's house next door. You see the family moved into my small trailer (thankfully I have a full foundation) so Susan could keep the house, while David was a way, it had to be rented out. They came to say good bye and let him know they would do their best to live up to his expectations. of them and try to accomplish what needed to be done. They had come to reassure. This was a blessing to have them as very young adults to make that commitment.

Finally, the lights were all shut out and we went to bed.

The tears now came quickly, and I could not stop them. I prayed and somehow, I fell asleep however brief and before I knew it, it was 1:00 in the morning. David's adopted dad was at the door promptly at 2:00 in the morning. He was always on time. He said he would drive. We were all a bit leery of his motive, but David wanted him there and decided that having someone to drive would be a good thing. We had divorced in 2002 and this was 2013.

David wanted to be a witness to his dad even though his dad had caused the hammer to drop hard on David's sentence. David forgave him, and so must I as my son said to me, 'Mom you have to forgive him, you just have to.' With every fiber of my being, I didn't want to and I wanted to hold in reserve of not letting go of the bitterness I felt. This was my son, my only son… How did God feel when everyone spat on His Son, mocked His Son, denied His Son and killed His Son? What right did I have to represent Jesus if I cannot forgive? Nothing goes by the Savior unless He allows it. He allowed it. Maybe a test for me to see if I am fit for His Kingdom.

The trip was a blur of darkness, city lights, then darkness again. David was talking with his dad, and my trying to stay awake and still get a nap. It was such a long ride. Susan and I lamented that we never saw the sunrise. Perhaps our eyes were closed, and we missed the whole thing. David's dad was in pain from his neck and David was getting weary. He and Susan exchanged seats and she drove for about 40 minutes when tiredness really was overtaking her. But David got 40 minutes of rest. I gave up my pillow so he would feel more comfortable. and I would have given up my life to have him safe. 'O dear God,' my cries were silent and excruciating within me, but I must not cry. I must not let him see my pain. He has enough of his own, so silently I let God know.

When David's dad finally took back over the driver's seat, and daylight was on us, the Tom-Tom GPS was outdated and telling us lefts when there weren't any and rights, when we knew better! It was beginning to be a tool of conversation and brought some light laughter. "First opportunity, turn around," it would say, and this would just bring on more criticism that made us laugh. However, we did have difficulty finding Ft Dix Federal Prison with the instructions of our GPS which did cause some apprehension. First, we went up one entrance to discover it was the wrong one. And again, it happened! David finally said, "That's it, if we don't find it this time, we will just go home." I am thankful for his sense of humor.

When we arrived at the right entrance, we knew it was the place we were looking for, and David promptly and adamantly said, "Mother don't cry.. It will make things harder for me.' On the heels of that command, he said, 'Susan don't cry.' I confidently assured him I would not. The guard said there was a sign over the door that said, 'Self-Surrender.' He was instructed to go there and take nothing with him. He passed Susan his list of names and addresses to be on his visitor's list and his money for commissary and took his meds with him, which he had, and walked alone to his destination as we watched from a distance. We stood watching, bravely with no tears visible only drowning within our hearts, and I broke the silence and said, "Let's pray before we leave.' With breaking hearts that only God could hear, the shattering of the fleshly pieces within my soul, I prayed with a cracking voice. I lifted my bowed head in time to see Dave, my x- husband, David's dad, wipe a falling tear from his cheek and Susan bracing herself for the ride home without her husband next to her.

The ride home went quite well, surprisingly. Dave and I reminisced our truck driving days in Canada, and all the funny things that happened to us. Susan sat in the back seat continuously redirecting the confused GPS and instructing Dave which way to go. He was getting confident in Susan's directions so when he was uncertain, he would call back to her for confirmation. Faith, Susan's daughter had been with the boys and many others rallied around to take the kids to Wal-Mart, McDonald's keeping them busy, and staying in touch with Susan so there were no worries. The pictures sent with their smiling faces displaced any negative thoughts and calmed our spirits.

It was bumper to bumper traffic through CT after breezing through the George Washington Bridge in NY, we rerouted to Route 91 then to Route 84 and missed the bottleneck traffic in MA. Connecticut was the only nightmare of travel back home.

I couldn't resist falling into lapses of sadness. Susan was being brave, and Dave was trying to be funny. We continued with light conversation trying not to think about thoughts of David and his painful night of being introduced to prison life. Now Dave was feeling his own pain, living with a woman who didn't want to serve God and he was realizing the seriousness of his situation. His depression reminded him of the depression I had gone through. He was softly telling me how he understood all that he had put me through and the years of depression I had suffered. I couldn't say anything back. I wanted to. I wanted to say, "You left me. You deserted me when I needed you most. I loved you so much, and I would have walked the ends of the earth for you to be the husband I loved. I had forgiven you for all your infidelity and longed for your healing and to make things right with the children you adopted. Why did you do this to me? to us?" But this was only said within my thoughts. I couldn't say anything. All the closeness of our moments together, flooded into my senses and I longed to have him hug me, but I knew I could never trust that intimacy again. never again could I be so hurt, I just couldn't, so now the emotions doubled, and the emotional pain was even greater. It came to me, how Christ must have felt when Judas betrayed Him, the hurt and pain realizing this man, He loved and was about to give His life for walked away from him forever.

There is no time to hold on to grudges or the what if's or the maybe's of life. Jesus is soon to return. Perhaps even before this book is published but if it is after a time, I pray that each one who reads these words will recognize the Love of God and there is no sin that is so tangled that God cannot untangle it. I look forward to the day when our Savior appears, and hear His words are 'Well done thou good and faithful servant…' (Matthew 25:23).

'Father, I lay my son in the cleft of the Rock
and cry out Teshuah! (deliverance).
Keep him safe and strengthen his mind as he dwells unknowingly,
in the refuge of Thy arms.'
Amen.

Justice vs Injustice

CHAPTER SEVENTEEN

"I know that whatever God does, it shall be forever,
Nothing can be added to it,
And nothing taken from it,
God does it and that men should fear before Him.
That which has already been, and what is to be has already been;
And God requires an account of that what is past."
Ecclesiastes 3:14-15 (NKJV)

While reviewing all that took place during the two years my son was in prison and all that my family endured during that time as well as all the intervention that was going on behind the scenes, I believe that God had His hand over us, and it became a way of being prepared for harder times. It was now 2018 and my son had been out of prison since 2015. He had six months of house arrest and wore an ankle bracelet. It was just good to have him home. However, getting into a working world after being so restricted as well as suffering from diabetes, high blood pressure and all that those things that inflict the human body which were not as they had once been in during his working world. He was able to get a street sweeper and it was his intent to rebuild a business, but this fell by the wayside, and we had to sell the street sweeper to make ends meet.

There were multiple challenges as we tried as a family to work together and all of us living in small home was a challenge in itself. It was October 7, 2018 in evening and we decided to have a bond fire and the kids could toast marshmallows. We had a lot of brush to be burned and so I obtained a fire permit from the town. It was not long into our evening with lawn chairs about the fire going with the kids running about, when a truck pulled in and two Forest Rangers jumped out and rushed over to the bond fire with a heat sensor to check our fire!

It seems a concerned citizen reported our bond fire! Our fire was within the proximity of boundaries so there was no violation and we had shovels, rakes, and garden hose all available. They found one piece of pressure treated wood about a foot long. That is a "no-no." My son said, to the officers, show me where it is, and I will take it out. That was done. They proceeded to take pictures of debris on the ground within the outskirts around the property that surrounded the bond fire of some metal debris that had fallen off the street sweeper. Those pictures were used as proof that we were violating the fire code. They asked to see the fire permit and I directed them to the front door where it was tacked because by now I was angry at their attitude and if they wanted to see it, then they could go look at it.

They asked why I got the permit and not my son. I answered, "Because I am the property owner." During our conversation, they asked the same question two more times. I gave them the same answer. The senior officer was evidently making me an example for the Rookie that he was training so gave me a ticket to go to court. Now I was irate and dumbfounded. He could have had a little more courtesy, but he told me I didn't need to go to court, that I could just call in and pay the fine.

It was my full intention to go to court as I felt this was an injustice. The Court date was scheduled for December 5, 2018. In the meantime, before the court date, I went to court with my son for his issues with his x-wife within the month of October. Then the month of November was birthdays and Thanksgiving. I also became very ill with the flu for almost 2 weeks. I totally forgot about the court date.

A December evening an officer came to my door and asked for "Joyce Leonard." I said I was she and he proceeded to tell me I was under attest! I was astonished and asked, "For what?" He then told me, "Failure to appear." I explained I had forgotten. He handcuffed me with my son pleading that he handcuff me in the front due to my many health issues with a rod in my back, plate in my neck and replaced knee and hip! He did. It was dark out when I was escorted to the SUV police car waiting for me. I needed help getting in and he refused, saying he could not do that. It was quite a struggle for me at 70 years old and my health issues. I began a conversation with the officer. He said he couldn't hear me as there was Plexiglas that was partially open between the front seat and back seat. I suppose with the sound of the car made it difficult for him to hear, so I leaned forward as much as I could and hollered as loud as I could, "Can you hear me now?" he affirmed he could, and I commenced to let him know of my situation.

At the police station, I was relieved of my outer clothing, boots and socks and had cardboard flip flops twice my size to wear as I stood in a designated, red-lined area while being processed. I was not made to wear one of their jumpsuits as they knew I had family coming to bail me out. I was put in the holding cell which had a wooden slatted bench supported against a cement wall. There was nothing warm in there on this December evening. There was Plexiglas windows on two sides of the cell so you could see out into the work area of the officers. A young woman was escorted in to wait with me in the holding cell and her crime was "theft." She had stolen some items for her children as she didn't have any money and was arrested. She volunteered her information to me, and I prayed with her. She was in shock that I was in there for a piece of wood being burned!

It was over a two hour wait for the Bail Bondsman. My only interruptions were to be fingerprinted, which turned out to be a challenge for the officers as they couldn't seem to get a good print. I told them it is because I do so many dishes! Then they had another challenge getting my photo. The camera wasn't working right. so it was a bit hazy but they called it good after several tries. I chuckled to myself that it was pay back for arresting me for such an injustice to begin with!

At last I was released into the comforting hands of my daughter-in-law and taken home where my grandsons wanted to know every detail of what I went through. My court date was scheduled for December 19, 2018. I had written up the entire incident and had a copy of it with me when I went to court. My name was not called, and I inquired with the Assistant DA as to why I was not called. She said she would look into it and after awhile she called me to her table and told me that they had forgotten to send the paperwork on me. I asked, "Are they going to be arrested?" She looked at me and asked what I meant. I said, "I had forgotten about the court date and I was arrested. They forgot to send the paperwork so should they not be arrested also?" Then she said would like to see the "lawyer of the day?" I immediately replied, "Yes, I would." The lawyer approached me and I passed him my written explanation of what had taken place. His words were, "Tell them to go to hell!" I retorted back to him, "No, that is your job." He spoke to the DA and then came and asked if I would be willing to make a charitable donation to an organization of my choice of $100? I asked, "Can it be my church?" He said "Yes." I agreed. I pay tithe and offering so it was not anything that do not already do, so I complied with the decision.

My name was in the paper and read by many who know me and quite taken back over the circumstances. It is my firm belief that whoever the "concerned citizen" was that reported our fire, which we had done this for years and never had any repercussions from burning brush or dead wood, that it was the intent to cause some issue for my son since he had been in prison. It was a suspicion of mine that since the Forest Ranger, Mr. M. had asked three times why I did not have my son acquire the fire permit that there was some underlying reason that the entire episode took place. Since they could find no other indication to arrest him, I was the target and made an example of what can be done by disobeying the law which had to be dealt with as a matter of justice. Oh yes, criminals need to be dealt with and justice must prevail.

The Word of God says, *"Mercy triumphs over justice."* (James 2:13) So does man make it his responsibility to triumph over mercy and make the determination to make a simple misdemeanor an unjust circumstance and diminish the credibility of some just citizens just because the law cries Justice? Yet, when an injustice comes into play, it is rarely made public and is there ever restitution? If the crime is one that is racial or of a greater magnitude, then the victims are avenged by whoever the perpetrator was, even within the justice system, individuals are brought to Justice for their injustice.

However, in a small community for an unknown citizen or one that is not of great wealth of circumstance, the injustice goes unheeded and no restitution is made to that one just person.

Think about it.

The day will come when "all manner of evil will be said about you falsely" (Matthew 5:11) and who will stand up for you? Not the Law of Justice. Only the law that believes in the Word of God and stands up for truth and will not back down regardless of the consequences for the day will come when the Lord will come and avenge His people when He comes in the clouds of glory. I pray you are ready to receive Him.

There is a Target on Your Back

CHAPTER EIGHTEEN

"The Lord knows how to rescue godly men from trials."
II Peter 2:9 (NIV)

When you have walked through the hot coals of life and found yourself in circumstances beyond your control and been found guilty once, then you are assumed to always be guilty becomes a battle one faces for a lifetime. I am most thankful that the God I serve doesn't work that way. When you have worked with Prison Ministry and written to numerous inmates, visited the State Prison, then been the upfront bystander watching the system with your own brother and then your son, you can begin to feel great compassion for those who are struggling to find themselves. Now since the ministry expanded to my home which began with the beginning of COVID that highlighted the process, then many facets of the trials began to unfold.

My heart longs to see the lost saved by the glorious power of my Savior Who still transforms and draws men and women in. The world throws them away, and it is the ones that feel the compelling desire to see them saved while walking the thin line to intercede for the fallen and when you do that, the enemy has a target on your back making you the suspicious one among those who are trying to control crime, so you are the one to attack and bring down.

Having said this, it has been my experience that there are good and bad on both sides of the law. Not all law enforcement is looking out for the welfare of others and then there are those who walk the extra mile with their lives being overtaken by the enemy. To the families of those, I say, Jesus is coming again, and He will avenge those who have lost much and restore what the enemy has stolen.

My journey continues with helping the helpless. I don't have wealth, but I have Jesus. I don't have great influence but I have the power of the Holy Spirit. I have more than most with just serving God who "supplies all my needs according to His riches in glory." (Philippians 4:19) My son came to me and asked if Mr. C could stay the night in my garage as he had no where to go. I said he could and so one night went into almost 2 weeks when we discovered Mr. C. was using a needle for his drug addiction and he was smoking. That in itself is a violation of my house rules. Having quit smoking over 40 years ago I do not allow smoking in my home and only in designated areas outside of my home. When I find a cigarette butt on the ground, it infuriates me. Birds take these and choke on the filters which destroys the life of the birds that come to my yard. I have made myself quite clear on this issue. My son has never smoked and suffers from asthma as I do so it is a health issue as well. I had a dear friend die of lung cancer caused from second hand smoke. I believe cigarettes are as much of a drug addiction and just as hard to overcome as any other drug out there – it is just legal and easily acquirable without law enforcement. When taking an EMT (Emergency Medical Technician) class I learned that alcohol is the number one drug and to get off the hold that alcohol claims is life threatening. Yet this too is a legal drug supported and used by some law enforcement officials without thought or concern.

When I learned about Mr. C. I confronted him when he came in and told him he had to leave that very night. I was not going to put myself in the position of having my garage burned down because he fell asleep with a cigarette or die from an overdose from using a needle to support his drug habit. My son found a temporary place for him to stay and within a couple weeks he ended up in the crisis unit, I have heard he was drug free and returned home with his mother and got his son back. I was thankful. I had given him a Bible and during the short time he was here we talked of spiritual things.

On the heels of Mr. C leaving, two ladies came with their broken-down car that needed repairs. They ended up staying quite awhile in my garage as they had nowhere to go and being winter at the time, they had lived in their car, I couldn't let them stay in a car for the winter. There were no accommodations in the upstairs of my garage, only an old mattress, warm blankets, and a heater. I ministered to them, and they were given Bibles. My son repaired the car and one left without warning. The other stayed and friends followed her to our house since it was fast becoming a safe haven. With each one that came, a Bible was given and some even took part in Bible studies.

There are always a few that take advantage of the situation as most have been former inmates and still under the rules that "there is no honor among thieves" they stole and used our inconvenient conveniences to their advantage. Oh yes, I was angry with particularly some of them and I let them know that they had a certain amount of time and they were to be gone. God has provided me with a demeanor of authority and a portion of holy discernment to be able to cope and see through some situations. I can love them but hate what they do and not allow them to control me. Some of those who came here really gripped hold of my heart strings and when they left a piece of me left too. I can only believe that the seeds dropped will be remembered and one day they will make that turn around before it is forever too late.

Some knew they overstepped my prerequisites and left before I could confront them. I was told by one who is here that I intimidate them if they don't really know my terms with wanting them to follow the right way. For some it is because they do not want me to think badly of them and don't want to disappoint me. This was not a decision to begin a place for the homeless, it was a design that God put in our path and we just followed the lead. It seems law enforcement didn't see it that way and since my son had a record and they assumed the worst. We had several visits from officers searching and handcuffing some of the residents here even my grandson, 19 who had issues of understanding and was totally innocent of any type of misbehavior. This disturbed me with a determination to have the record set straight and I suppose in writing this, I am attempting to set that record straight. When I fight, it is with the power of the pen.

The men who wandered here we had helped with different things that would better their living conditions. We used their talents to help since they paid no rent of any sort. My brother also in the homeless mode moved here with his van parked on the further end of my property and used as a place to sleep. He has many abilities for survival and uses them to his advantage as he likes to be alone.

The plan was to have a place of business to do mechanic work even if we did not have a sign to advertise but work came by word of mouth. We learned of complaints that were made from a source unknown to us of what we were doing, and Code Enforcement was called. They surveyed my property telling me I was only allowed such and such and then to have people living within the garage I needed other provisions as well. This all costs mosey we haven't had and with my son's physical disabilities and my daughter-in-law unable to work due to different physical problems we had limited provisions. Doing labor here and there with vehicles has helped with what we haven't had.

God continues to supply our needs as well as we have received a few donations to help with the ministering we are doing. A dry camper was given to us and it became a place to stay in for two of our homeless and then they transferred to the garage and the camper was given to a couple that stayed here with no place to go. They have since left and the Camper was given to them. A RV was also given to us for use for the homeless and it was repaired so it can be used for others when the ones that were in it left. Just when you think down-sizing has begun and there is noone who has made any great commitments to God in the process, then someone returns, or another comes back and asks for forgiveness.

We have had two stable ones that have stayed and are learning about Jesus. It is a test of patience. One attends church and his faith is being tested with throat cancer. Before learning this, we had officers that sat in the parking lot next door to my home facing our direction and turning their siren on occasionally to cause irritation, or a scare tactic or whatever it may be called. They waited till late at night and sat across the road from my property with their headlights blaring on my property should anyone leave since everyone stayed up late on a Saturday night working in the garage, they would follow them. These Officers were overheard saying to someone at the local variety store in town that they were having a "little fun" as they ordered pizza and sandwiches laughing at their scheme to continue their harassment in their nightly surveillance.

This was only one of many incidents that occurred. The last one was when my son was stopped here in town and he wasn't driving but the officers made him get out of the car and take off his shoes while he stood on the pavement in stocking feet, then they squeezed his toes causing such pain since he suffers from neuropathy in his feet. They reached in and illegally took his wallet off the dash to check it out. I was angered by this when it was relayed to me, and I prepared a letter for the Attorney General. I never sent it as my son said to "wait." I did but I include the letter in this writing.

Time is short dear reader, when the issues of life will be brought before each of us. It was not until I voiced my thoughts to let the Chief of Police to know that I have kept a journal for the last 35 years and I know from prior experience that a journal is considered evidence within the court of law. I keep an account of all that happens every day alongside my prayer journal.

You can play with people's lives and think you are making a difference when you keep the law. And you are. But are you also keeping the Law of God? I have discovered that those who have come to my home with no where to go and want to be drug free don't know anything about Jesus. They are searching for something better. Some are willing to do whatever it takes to make the difference within themselves and there are others that have wallowed in sin for so long, that it has become comfortable to them, so they keep going back to it. Some have never held a Bible and some have no idea that the truths within the pages are the truths that can set them free. They can truly come out of the darkness and have… "Freedom Within."

(Note) The following letter that *was not sent* to the Attorney General's Office as the issue that was suppose to appear in court was removed without the issue going to the Attorney General's Office.

TO: Office of the Attorney General Department of Justice
111 Sewell St.
Augusta, ME 04330

This complaint encompasses the Rights of a citizen, the harassment of law officers and going forward with legal counsel if necessary.

On **August 22, 2022,** my son, _____ had just gone to NAPA for parts for my car that was needed for repairs to be able to use it. He was accompanied by _____ who lives here within the confines of my home and property. Mr. M is on probation with no restrictions on record. Mr. M was driving the leased car from Enterprise Rental. They were pulled over just after leaving the town inner limits heading out on So. Main St. in Mechanic Falls. No reason was given for the pull-over. Mr. M was asked to get out of the car and searched without permission. My son, the passenger was also asked to do the same. He questioned the officer and asked why the officer needed to inquire of him since he was not driving, and the demand followed his question with "get out." He did and they took his wallet and searched as well as handcuffing him and making him take off his sneakers and stand by the roadside for up to an hour in his stocking feet. He explained to them he has neuropathy in his feet. They ignored it, and squeezed his feet, causing extreme pain. He also has neuropathy in his hands and that made no difference. He is a diabetic and this was an abuse of force as well as an assault on my son's person on the part of the officers.

There was no probable cause for the pull-over and the harassment that follows from the harassment that happened on **June 18, 2022** at my home. *That write up is also included in this report*. They took both Mr. M and my son in separate vehicles bringing them back and taking the leased car to Enterprise Rental to get permission to search it. There was nothing found. (The Supreme Court Monday said that just because the name of a driver of a rental car is not on the rental agreement, that does not automatically mean that he or she has diminished privacy rights), Washington CNN

May 2018 This law was passed recently.

Arriving at my home was a barrage of officers suited for action. They searched the garage where Mr. M sleeps and then came out. No search warrant was obtained. I house homeless and those who have been incarcerated and have problems and are trying to have a better lifestyle. I have four such ones here presently. I have had up to 8 at one time. Some have made their way out to other living places. Some were asked to leave as they did not want to follow the house rules here. I have been in Prison Ministry from 1998—2004. My health caused me to let go of the Ministry "Freedom Within." Yet I continue to write to several inmates and send them encouragement and Bible study.

My son was incarcerated in 2013-2015 for dealing drugs—nonviolent. It seems since his release in 2015 there seems to be a vendetta against him, and it began when I was burning brush and such in 2018 when two wardens came and used a detector to see what was in the fire. They found a piece of wood a foot long that was pressure treated. They were disturbed that it was me who obtained the fire permit and asked three times why my son didn't get the permit. I reiterated each time that it was my property, and it is the duty of the property owner to get the permit. I was fined.

It seems as if my son is being made an example of some sort and I find this is not only unjust and illegal but also quite distressing as I also have twin grandsons that live here that are now 12 years old. I have a 19-year-old grandson with challenges so these harassment measures are very disturbing to these children and my 19 year old grandson who has struggled with being able to cope after being emotionally controlled by his mother.

State Trooper JW seems to be able to get his way with issues and uses his authority abusively. I know how enforcement can work. I am not impressed with his deliberate harassment tactics. Since there was illegal searches and illegal entries and abusive force and discrimination used on my son, causing him to have to stay in bed the entire day following this incident due to the force of having him stand on the tar with stocking feet and having his feet squeezed in the condition they are in, was not called for under any measures. I feel at the very least a reprimand should be made on his call to control the involvement of those who were called unnecessarily to my home.

I respectfully submit this report and I hope it is taken seriously because of the nature of the situation here and trying to help people this is not discarded as a disgruntled mother for her son. This has affected everyone here on this property as well as my neighbors.

I am including the full report of the harassment on June 18, 2022, as well as that of October 13, 2018 that I feel is part of the ongoing harassment which seems to be continuing. There is also an available witness for this last incident who watched officers reach in through the car window to take things off the dash and were witness to the assault on my son's feet. All reports are journaled and available as evidence, if necessary, in a court of law.

Respectfully,
Joyce A. Leonard

> *"And shall God not avenge His own elect who*
> *cry out day and night to Him,*
> *though He bears long with them?*
> *I tell you that He will avenge them speedily. Nevertheless,*
> *when the Son of Man comes, will He really find faith on the earth?"*
> *Luke 18:7-8 (NKJV)*

> *"Is this not the fast I have chosen,*
> *To loose the bonds of wickedness, to undo the heavy burdens,*
> *To let the oppressed, go free,*
> *And that you break every yoke?*
> *Is it not to share your bread with the hungry,*
> *And to bring to your house the poor that are cast out,*
> *When you see the naked, that you cover him,*
> *And not hide yourself from your own flesh?"*
> *Isaiah 58:7-8 (NKJV)*

I end this writing with a salute to those who walk a difficult path pertaining to justice and walking under the scrutiny of facing challenges that are extremely difficult, who protect with their own life and do not take advantage of those who are less fortunate but are willing to give them another chance, and carefully judge with a clear conscience. Those who see the scenes of horror and have to relive it over and over again each time they close their eyes. To you who are honest in heart, I thank you for your courage to stand against the odds and consider it a privilege and an honor to serve God first and your country. *God bless you.*

Not Everyone

Dear Father in heaven,
Not everyone wants to walk and talk Jesus.
Not everyone craves His presence.
Not everyone has interest in the Creator,
And not everyone cares about salvation.
But Father in Your great mercy,
Who sees what I cannot,
And has emotions like I do,
Because I am created in Your image.,
And Your divine Spirit moves,
Just because I long to see,
And continue to pray,
For those around me to be saved.
I believe my prayer moves Your arm.
For under the great Rock of ages
Stands hope, stands repentance.
And You are ever calling.
Conviction stirs in the coldest of hearts,
And tears flow because of Your great Love
That calls the sinner out of darkness…
Into "Freedom Within."

Joyce A. Leonard

"There is Nothing New Under the Sun"

What calamities invade the soul of a man?
And provoke the unheard of. . . or are they?
Grief strikes and how does one respond.
To life's unraveling strands of array?
With dignity the head bowed low,
Plugging on – just waving it aside, you know
And the world looks on and shakes their heads.
How could they, - why would they?
As questions without answers begin to grow.

One sips silently the swirling, numbing killer,
in the darkness of the night,
Raging inside, feeling alone and desperate,
despicable in his own sight.
While on the other side of town a mother leaves her children
to the plight of another or even death.
How could she. . . a mother.

A man molests a child,
Rapes and mangles and mutilates the gift of life.
A man married with a wife. . . and yet –
"There is nothing new under the sun,"
Where life twists and turns and sends man on the run.

A thief enters and steals what isn't his,
While another steals emotion with lustful eyes and sweet lies.
A murderer takes life blood and splatters it on the ground.
He buries his prey hoping never to be found.
He drinks from the cup of vile,
Filling his heart with deceit all the while.

A woman warms the bed of her best friends' husband,
And laughs with her friend in denial.
Cruelty rages on every side from verbal abuse to drug use.

Sexual immorality, to emotional infidelity. . . .
Turmoil of every sort known to man
As meaningless acts engage the mind.
To scoff the Christian values, while trauma lingers
And where grief fills the mind.
The emptiness of love and all those excuses they can find.
Ending in horrors unspeakable while others are shaking their fist.
When they themselves are walking in the midst
Of their own deceit and covered ways,
Acting and reacting with amaze,
"For there is nothing new under the sun,"
Where life twists and turns and sends man on the run.

Which is the worst sin my friend?
The one that cannot be forgiven in the end.
Which one bears the death penalty?
And then
What about the one who overindulges,
Who eats till they are sick and their belly bulges?
Who spits their food out after a binge,
While others shake their heads and cringe.
And then the intemperance of burning the midnight oil,
And battering their body with willful piercings under ugly toil.
What about them?
Criticizing and gossiping about the nasty ways and deeds of another.
The beating father and the slothful mother
Are these just simple sins?
Sins that were all bought without a price,
Oh no. . . .
They were paid with blood with the ultimate sacrifice.
For it cost heaven a hefty price.

And who are you to chide heaven away –
To deny the battle on Calvary's cross and all that happened that day.
And who are you to kick at heaven's door?
To shake your fist and spew your anger sore?

And who are you to laugh off eternity?
Are your sins less and your heart all pure?
Are you ready for your trials alone to endure?
"There is nothing new under the sun,"
Where life twists and turns and sends man on the run.

When you judge another, criticizing with contempt,
Does that make you holy and exempt?
You have taken part in the murder of a mind,
Where imagination soars and negativity can bind,
For you contributed to molesting dreams and hopes that are dashed,
Where hurt is rehearsed and thrashed.
When you say more than you know for a fact,
You are keeping a lie intact.
Inferring more than you should,
And not providing the propensity for good,
For you are taking part in the death of someone's heart.
"For there is nothing new under the sun,"
Where life twists and turns and sends man on the run.

This is why Jesus must come,
To save those who have suffered and some
Who have been pure in heart,
And waited patiently from the start.
To save the unlovely lives that have been redeemed,
For they repented and paid the consequences
of what mercies esteemed.
He must save those who long for salvation on the heavenly shore,
To say farewell to sin forever more.
To save those who have been forgiven,
And want their sins forever blotted out.
Because they believe without doubt.
Those who long for love that was never returned,
Love that was jeered and spurned.
These are those who are willing to stand fast,
For the power of redemption to draw nigh at last,

Out of the Darkness... "Freedom Within"

As they cry out in their sorrow to their God on high.
"For there is nothing new under the sun,"
For life twists and turns and sends man on the run.
By Joyce A. Leonard written 09/15/2008
Inspired after a conversation with Katherine Harnett Hall Delan Jones